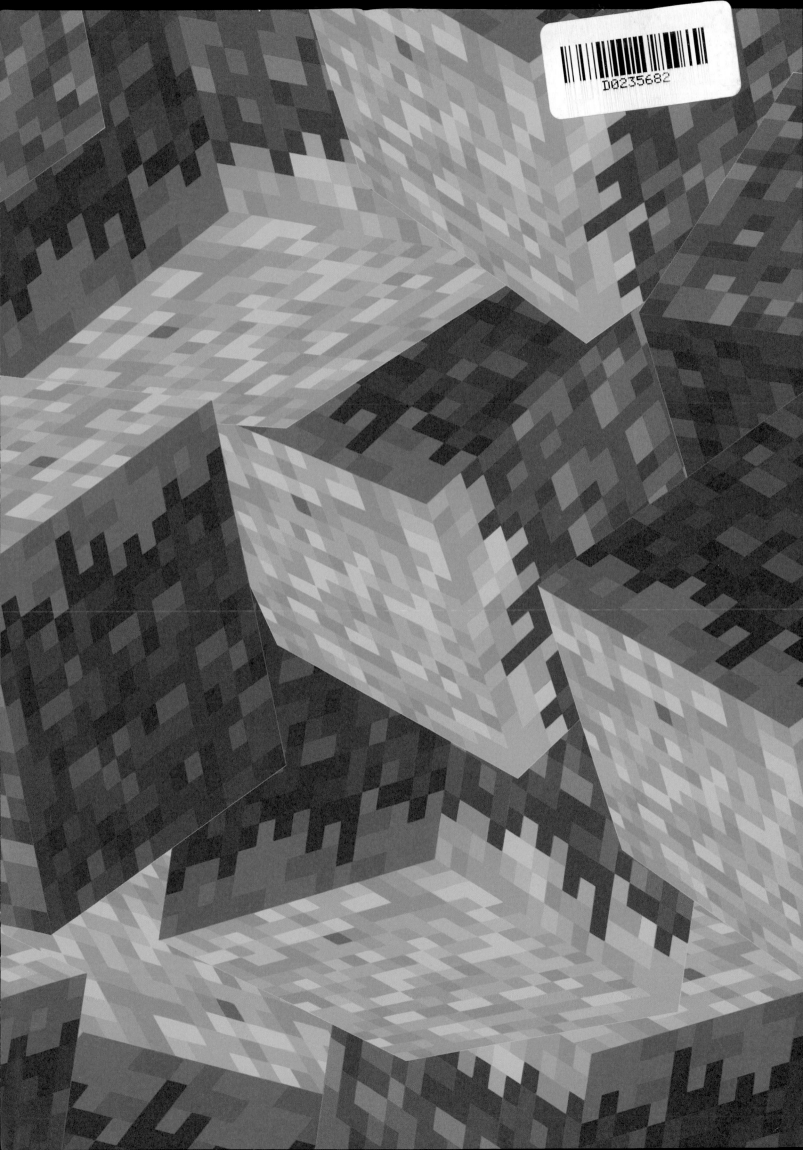

GAMES MASTER

PRESENTS

MINECRAFT

PUZZLES

Learn the Minecraft Basics

PAGE **6**

Everything you ever wanted to ask about your favourite game in one place!

PAGE **40** THE BEST MINECRAFT PETS

Published 2019

Little Brother Books Ltd
Ground Floor, 23 Southernhay
East, Exeter, Devon, EX1 1QL

Printed in Poland

books@littlebrotherbooks.co.uk
www.littlebrotherbooks.co.uk

LittleBrother

BUILD A GINGERBREAD HOUSE!

PAGE 46

FOLLOW OUR STEP-BY-STEP INSTRUCTIONS – IT'S GOOD ENOUGH TO EAT!

PAGE
60
TRY OUR MINECRAFT QUIZ

PAGE
66
A CHAT WITH STAMPY LONGNOSE!

Inside...

THIS BOOK IS PACKED WITH HOURS OF MINECRAFT FUN!

THE PERFECT PLACE TO START YOUR MINECRAFT JOURNEY!

MASTER THE BASICS!

So you've survived your first night? Now it's time to get your teeth into Minecraft for real!

MAYBE YOU picked up this guide because you love Minecraft: you've been playing for ages and can't get enough of the game's blocky goodness! In that case, treat this basics section as a refresher course in your favourite game — give it a skim, then jump ahead to more challenging pages later on.

But if you're reading because you've heard your friends talking about Minecraft and want to join in, or you've already taken your first, perilous steps into blockland but were totally lost, get studying.

Minecraft is a complex game, which doesn't do much to ease new players in. To live a long, full life in your pixely new surroundings, you need to know how to craft items, breed animals, deal with monsters, and more.

It can be overwhelming, so we've made it simple — on the pages ahead you'll find everything you need to know to not only survive, but to start the long journey to becoming a Minecraft master. Turn the pages for tips on crafting your first bits of gear, Minecraft zoology, monster control, potion brewing, and much, much more.

CRAFTING GUIDE
EQUIPMENT & MATERIALS

IF YOU'VE survived your first night you're now ready to get cracking on the 'craft' portion of Minecraft. This guide will provide a handy reference to most of the basic materials and recipes you'll need for a strong start come your first morning. Tools, weapons and armour are some of the most fundamental items you can make in Minecraft. They're constructed from different materials you can harvest around the game, which influence their durability and effectiveness. Before you start crafting stuff, take a look at what you will need to gather from around the many Minecraft biomes...

1

WOOD

WOOD CAN be found on the surface in almost every biome you visit in the game (with deserts being a notable exception), and is needed for almost any basic recipe. It is the second-weakest material for making tools and weapons, yielding a sword that will break after dealing about 400 points of damage.

2

STONE

FOR BEGINNER miners, stone is the most common block to find beneath the surface, and can often be found above ground as well. You can use it to construct medium durability tools and weapons. A stone sword, for instance will break after dealing about 1000 points of damage – more than twice the strength of wood.

3

GOLD

SHINY GOLD is a rare ore found only in the lowest 32 layers of the world, meaning you'll have to dig for a while to find it. It is the weakest material to make tools, weapons, and armour from, so don't be tempted. Instead, save it for more valuable projects such as making clocks and powered minecart rails.

4

IRON

THIS IS a sturdy, uncommon material that can be found underground up to 63 layers above bedrock, meaning you shouldn't have to dig too deep underground to find it. It yields a sword that will break after dealing about 2200 points of damage, and is a good staple material to rely on for most tools and buildings.

5

DIAMOND

THIS PRECIOUS ore can only be found in the bottom eight layers of the map. It can take hours to find enough diamond to craft with, but it's worth it. Why? Well, a diamond sword will dish out about 16,000 points of damage without breaking, and a diamond pick can break any block type except obsidian in under one second.

1

TORCH

1 WOODEN STICK + 1 COAL

An essential piece of kit, torches are among the most important tools in the game for one reason: they prevent most nasty monsters from spawning. The coal component can be mined, or created in a furnace by burning uncut wood.

2

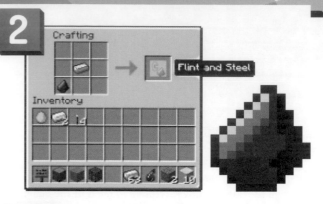

FLINT

1 FLINT + 1 STEEL INGOT

Other than by pouring buckets of lava on everything like a crazy caveman, which is quite dangerous, flint and an iron ingot are what you'll need to light things on fire in Minecraft. The flint in the recipe can be earned by breaking gravel blocks with a shovel.

3

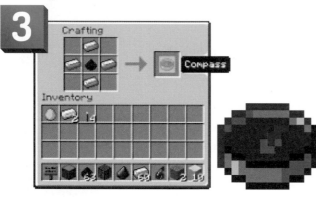

COMPASS

1 REDSTONE + 4 IRON INGOTS

A compass will point you toward your original spawn point in the game, which can be useful for finding your way back to your home base when hopelessly lost. Redstone can be found in ore veins deep underground – you will need to be in the bottom 16 levels of the map.

4

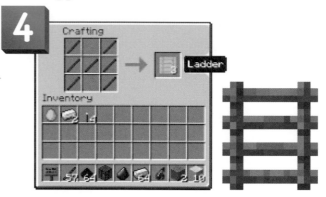

LADDER

7 WOODEN STICKS

Each time you craft this recipe using your collection of sticks you will produce three sections of ladder, which can be placed against a flat surface to assist in climbing. This is especially helpful as a quick way to the surface when exploring caves.

5

HELMET

5 LEATHER, CHAINMAIL, IRON, DIAMOND OR GOLD

Armour reduces the damage you take from enemy attacks. A helmet provides 1-3 points of protection. Pumpkins can also be equipped as helmets, but they don't have any armour value. They don't take damage either, though, so you can be a pumpkin head forever.

6

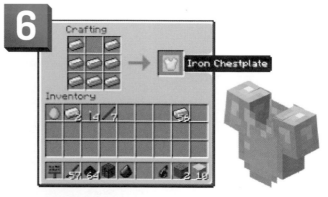

CHESTPLATE

8 LEATHER, CHAINMAIL, IRON, DIAMOND OR GOLD

A chestplate provides 3-8 points of protection and might save your life when a monster catches you off-guard. If you use leather, it'll be called a 'tunic'. In fact, all leather armour except boots has a different name: 'cap' instead of 'helmet' and 'pants' instead of 'leggings'.

7

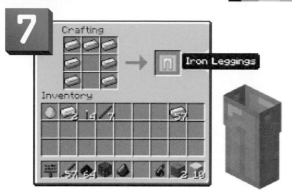

LEGGINGS

7 LEATHER, CHAINMAIL, IRON, DIAMOND OR GOLD
Leggings provide 2-6 points of protection against anything bad coming at you. Nothing about 'iron leggings' sounds very comfortable or practical, but your mobility won't be hindered by stomping around in solid metal trousers, thankfully.

8

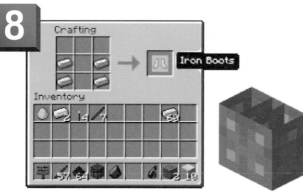

BOOTS

4 LEATHER, CHAINMAIL, IRON, DIAMOND OR GOLD
Boots provide 1-3 points of protection for your Steve or Alex. It's also a generally good idea to have a nice, comfortable pair of boots for adventuring, unless you want pixel blisters. (That doesn't really happen in Minecraft – it's just good life advice.)

FULL DIAMOND & ANVIL

BOOSTING YOUR ARMOUR Once you're fully decked out in diamond, you can have as much as 20 points of armour. That's enough to reduce all enemy damage by 80%! Armour and weapons degrade over time, though, so you may want to build an anvil (4 iron ingots, 3 iron blocks), which allows you to use raw materials to repair the durability of your items.

ARMOURED HORSE Horse armour can be crafted or you can find it in dungeons, temples, Nether fortresses, and NPC villages. It will offer your faithful steed 3-11 points of protection and, more importantly, help its regalia match your own.

I'M A LITTLE HORSE. I'VE BEEN SHOUTING ALL DAY!

ANIMAL GUIDE HOW TO BE A FARMER

ANIMAL BREEDING is a crucial skill in Minecraft thanks to all the resources it provides. Cows produce milk and leather, chickens produce eggs and feathers. And cows, chickens AND pigs also produce delicious, delicious meat. Breeding animals out in the open is difficult, so the first step towards a successful breeding program is to build a ranch. With a little bit of planning and a whole lot of fences, you can set up a ranch that provides you with plenty of animals. Here's how:

1

BUILD YOUR PEN

START WITH the classic animal pen by fencing off a big square area. Add a gate so you can walk in and out, obviously. A shallow pit (two blocks deep) can also keep animals inside. Don't forget a ladder so you can climb out and don't dig deep enough to hurt the animals when you push them in.

2

FIND YOUR HERD

FIND AN animal you would like to see in your farm out in the wild. Sheep are the easiest to work with — they love wheat and will follow you around when you're holding it. Lead your collected sheep back to your pen — slowly, since sheep are pretty stupid. Now go find another animal of the same species.

3

FEED THE ANIMALS

WITH YOUR wheat in hand, select each sheep and feed them one at a time. After their bellies are full, red hearts will start to float out of the sheep. That's a sign that they're feeling frisky. Now that they've been fed, the animals will lose interest in you. But that's okay: your job is done.

4

BABY ANIMALS

THE SHEEP will snuggle for about two seconds before as if by magic, a big-headed lamb will appear. Wow, that was quick! All baby animals will be smaller version of their parents, except with comically large heads. If you hold food the babies will follow you around. Dawwww! Oh, and baby lambs are scrummy!

5

GROW YOUR HERD

REPEAT THE process above to collect more sheep. After about five minutes you can breed the animals again. After about 20 minutes, the lamb will become an adult and be ready to breed itself. If you keep at it, you'll increase your herd over and over again. Don't forget to use your herd for food and resources!

ANIMAL PLANET

A **QUICK**-glance guide to Minecraft's main creatures and what they can give you if you harvest them!

1 SHEEP

- **RESOURCES:** Wool
- **EATS:** Grass Blocks, Wheat
- **FOUND:** Everywhere

2 COW

- **RESOURCES:** Raw Steak, Leather, Milk
- **EATS:** Wheat
- **FOUND:** Everywhere

3 CHICKEN

- **RESOURCES:** Raw Chicken, Feathers, Eggs
- **EATS:** Seeds
- **FOUND:** Everywhere

4 PIG

- **RESOURCES:** Raw Pork, Transportation (if saddled)
- **EATS:** Carrots
- **FOUND:** Everywhere

5 HORSE

- **RESOURCES:** Leather, Transportation (if tamed and saddled)
- **EATS:** Sugar, Wheat, Apple, Golden Apple, Golden Carrot, Hay Bale
- **FOUND:** Plains, Savannas

6 WOLF

- **RESOURCES:** Protection (if tamed)
- **EATS:** Raw Meat
- **FOUND:** Forest & Taiga

7 OCELOT

- **RESOURCES:** Tame Cat (when fed)
- **EATS:** Raw Fish
- **FOUND:** Jungle

8 MOOSHROOM

- **RESOURCES:** Mushrooms, Leather, Beef
- **EATS:** Wheat
- **FOUND:** Mushroom

9 SQUID

- **RESOURCES:** Ink Sac
- **EATS:** Who knows?
- **FOUND:** Rivers, Oceans & Beaches

POTIONS GUIDE

BREWING POTIONS is one of the most useful advanced disciplines to learn in Minecraft. The recipes may seem simple, but most will require you to search the far-flung corners of the Overworld and the Nether, slaying and sidestepping dangerous creatures. Here's how:

I LIKE TO BREW POTIONS... BUT MY NAME IS NOT HARRY!

1

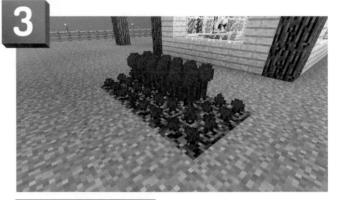

SETTING UP

TO GET yourself started in the art of brewing potions in Minecraft you need to make yourself a brewing stand, a cauldron and a lot of glass bottles. Fill the cauldron with water, transfer that water over to three bottles and then pop them into the stand. Right, now you're ready to start concocting some cool stuff!

2

CONSERVING INGREDIENTS

WHERE POSSIBLE, fill the brewing stand with bottles. Potions aren't expensive to make, but when each ingredient distils into three bottles, it's silly to waste space in your cool Minecraft home. Stick a stack of sand in a furnace to ensure you have enough glass for the bottles you want to make.

3

WARTS AND ALL

NETHER WART turns water bottles into Awkward Potions, the awkwardly named base for all the best effects in Minecraft. You can find Nether Wart growing naturally in the fortresses of The Nether. Bring back some Soul Sand too, as you can use it to plant a Nether Wart garden for an infinite supply.

4

BASIC ALCHEMY

FOR AN instant healing potion, add a Glistering Melon — created by combining a slice of melon with a gold nugget. Drinking these will restore two hearts each, though there are more efficient ways of getting back into fighting shape if you're patient enough... Swap out the Glistering Melon for a Ghast Tear, and you'll get a Potion of Regeneration that will heal you for one heart every two and a half seconds for 45 seconds. This is vastly superior for lengthy combat.

Getting those Ghast Tears is tough, and it'll take serious speed to harvest them without dying. A simple brew of sugar will create a Potion of Swiftness, increasing your speed, jumping power and field of vision for three minutes. If you're just looking for more stopping power, brew up some Blaze Powder for a Potion of Strength, which more

than doubles the power of every melee attack you make. You should be more than ready to take the fight to the deepest chasms. But don't leave without a Potion of Night Vision, allowing you to raid the monsters where they live without hauling lots of torches along. You can brew one using a golden carrot, which is made by crafting a normal carrot encircled by eight gold nuggets.

5

KICKING IT UP A NOTCH

STANDARD POTIONS not doing it for you? Adding a third ingredient to a pre-brewed potion can give you an even more potent effect.

Weaponize any potion by adding a creeper's gunpowder as an ingredient. It will create a splash potion, which can be fired like any ranged weapon for area-of-effect of devastating debuffs or, if you're playing with friends, helpful group healing.

Give yourself some extra time to breathe by adding Redstone Dust to any potion with a limited duration, increasing the time for the effect to wear off.

Glowstone Dust, harvested from Glowstone found in the Nether, can amplify the potency of a potion, but it also reduces the duration. For example, adding Glowstone dust to a Potion of Regeneration will double the rate of regeneration it grants you, but also cuts the duration to 16 seconds.

Fermented Spider Eye, which is exactly what it sounds like, will reverse the effect of a potion in some way. Adding it to a Potion of Healing will create a Potion of Harming... which can be combined with gunpowder to make a damaging grenade. Adding it to a Potion of Night Vision will create a Potion of Invisibility.

BAKE A CAKE!

BUILD BUCKETS
Ingredients: 3 iron ingots per bucket

First, you'll need to make three iron buckets (a total of nine ingots) to collect milk. Milk, of course, comes from cows, which can be found in just about any biome with lots of grass. Just interact with the cow using the bucket to get milk.

Next, you'll need eggs, which spawn under chickens. You should be able to find chickens in the same general areas as cows.

Finally, you're going to need some wheat. First, find some tall grass and punch it until you get some seeds. Once you have your seeds, it's time to craft a hoe so you can harvest your wheat.

CRAFT A HOE
Ingredients: 2 wooden sticks + 2 iron ingots

We've used iron, but you can also make a hoe with wood planks, stone, gold, or diamond. Use the hoe on the ground to create farmland, then select the turf with your seeds to plant them. The wheat will take a while to grow — it will need light, and will grow faster if it is within a couple of tiles of a water block.

Lastly, you'll need some sugar, which is crafted from sugar cane. You should be able to find sugar cane growing along most large rivers and lakes.

Once you have all the ingredients ready, it's off to the kitchen!

BAKE THE CAKE
Ingredients: 3 buckets of milk + 2 sugar + 1 egg + 3 wheat

Behold! Cake! Each cake is good for 6 servings, which will restore one point of hunger. See! It isn't a lie!

MONSTER GUIDE

EXPLORING THE dark corners of Minecraft risks death at the blocky fists of many nasty beasts. Your most important weapon in the fight for survival is knowledge in terms of which creatures might be lurking around the next bend in the cave. And how to deal with them! Study this monster guide well...

AARRRGHHH! I HATE MONSTERS! THEY KEEP ME AWAKE AT NIGHT!

1

ZOMBIE

HEALTH: 10 **EXP:** 5

ENCOUNTERED: In low light: the overworld after sun down, poorly-lit structures and caves. So, everywhere.

SPECIAL ABILITIES: If a villager mob is killed by a zombie, it can rise as a hostile zombie villager. You will also occasionally run into zombies with weapons and armour – so watch out.

WEAKNESSES: Like all undead, zombies burn up in sunlight. They also move very slowly. An iron sword and armour should be more than enough, depending on whether or not the zombie has equipment of its own. Bows also work, as zombies have no ranged attack.

2

SPIDER

HEALTH: 16 **EXP:** 5

ENCOUNTERED: Spiders only spawn in low-light areas, but can wander out into the sun without taking damage.

SPECIAL ABILITIES: Spiders can climb up smooth walls and fit inside two-block-wide by one-block-high openings, which the player and other mobs can't. This is important to know when designing shelters. Spiders also have a lunging jump attack that can catch you off guard.

WEAKNESSES: Bows are a good way to deal with spiders, since engaging them close-up puts you in range of their jump attack. It's also possible to knock one off of a surface while it's climbing, and let the fall damage do the work. Spiders can also become non-hostile if exposed to direct sunlight.

VARIANTS: A more dangerous version of this mob, the Cave Spider, only spawns deep underground. It's bluish in colour, small enough to fit through one-by-one openings, and its bite is highly poisonous. Bring milk (which can cure poisoning) if you think you might be exploring in cramped, underground areas on your Minecraft adventures.

3

BLAZE

HEALTH: 10 **EXP:** 10

ENCOUNTERED: Only in Nether Fortresses.

SPECIAL ABILITIES: While not as tough as a ghast, they are much faster and smaller (making them harder to hit). They shoot non-explosive fire projectiles at you in quick, machine-gun-like bursts. Getting hit by these projectiles will, understandably, set you alight.

WEAKNESSES: Know that saying about "a snowball's chance in hell?" When you're fighting blazes, that chance is actually pretty good. Weaponized snow doesn't hurt as much as arrows, but can be fired much faster. And since you'll need to duck in and out of cover a lot to avoid the blaze's attacks, packing powder is a great technique.

4

SKELETON

HEALTH: 10 **EXP:** 5

ENCOUNTERED: Skeletons spawn in the same conditions as zombies.

SPECIAL ABILITIES: Skeletons come equipped with a bow, allowing them to attack you from range with terrifying accuracy. You might also encounter one riding on the back of a spider. Beware the bone cavalry!

WEAKNESSES: As undead creatures, skeletons burn up in sunlight. If death by solar radiation isn't an option, it's best to meet them on their own terms with either a bow or thrown potions, as getting close enough to attack with a sword and not being hit by arrows can be challenging.

VARIANTS: A special type of skeleton called a Wither Skeleton only spawns in fortresses deep in the Nether dimension. They carry swords instead of bows, and their attacks can place a damaging curse on you.

5

ZOMBIE PIGMAN

HEALTH: 10 **EXP:** 5

ENCOUNTERED: Zombie pigmen only spawn in the Nether dimension, and usually in groups.

SPECIAL ABILITIES: ZPs come armed with a sword, and are the only undead mob that doesn't burn up in sunlight. Like wolves, attacking one of them will alert all of its nearby friends to come to its aid.

WEAKNESSES: If you can't just avoid them, fighting zombie pigmen is almost the same as fighting plain old zombies, but their attacks do much more damage to you. Before the battle starts, make sure you have a narrow place to retreat to so they can't all gang up on you from different angles.

6

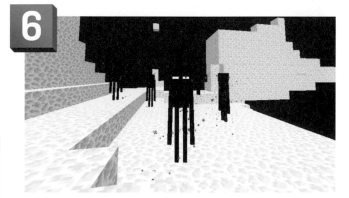

ENDERMAN

HEALTH: 20 **EXP:** 5

ENCOUNTERED: Endermen spawn in the same conditions as zombies – albeit rarely – and frequently in The End.

SPECIAL ABILITIES: Endermen can pick up and move blocks, as well as teleport great distances in any direction. They can usually teleport away faster than you can strike at them, and will tend to appear behind you for a sneak counter-attack.

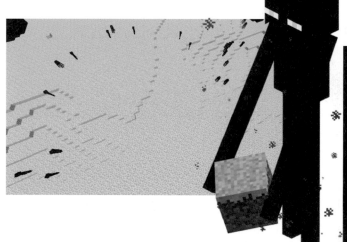

WEAKNESSES: Endermen generally mind their own business and only attack if you attack first or if you look directly at them. Their biggest weakness is water. They will usually be killed if caught out in a rainstorm, and will retreat if the player hides in a lake or river. Their size means they can't follow you into a space less than three blocks high. If you're eager to look, wear a pumpkin on your head.

7

8

CREEPER

- **HEALTH:** 10 ▪ **EXP:** 5

- **ENCOUNTERED:** Minecraft's most iconic mad bombers spawn in the same low-light conditions as zombies.

- **SPECIAL ABILITIES:** A creeper's special ability is also, sort of, a weakness. Its only means of attack is moving right up next to the player and blowing itself up. They can often catch you unaware, as they are completely silent until just before they detonate. Hssssss...

- **WEAKNESSES:** If a creeper never gets close enough to detonate, it's harmless. Ranged weapons are useful, but the best defense is being aware of your surroundings and making sure your bases are well-lit enough so they don't have anywhere to spawn.

WITCH

- **HEALTH:** 13 ▪ **EXP:** 5

- **ENCOUNTERED:** Witches dwell in witch huts, which only appear in swamp biomes.

- **SPECIAL ABILITIES:** Minecraft Witches make use of potions, allowing them to heal themselves while damaging and debuffing the player. They can also increase their own speed and become immune to fire.

- **WEAKNESSES:** Witches have no melee attack, and their potions have a much shorter range than a bow. Ranged combat is your best bet, and be sure to bring some helpful potions of your own (although offensive ones will not be effective).

9

WOLF

- **HEALTH:** 8 ▪ **EXP:** 1-3

- **ENCOUNTERED:** Wolves usually spawn in packs in forested areas, and can spawn at any time of day.

- **SPECIAL ABILITIES:** Wolves are very fast, and have a forward leap attack much like a spider. If one wolf in a group is angered, the rest of the pack will help it deal with the threat.

- **WEAKNESSES:** Wolves aren't hostile to players unless attacked. In fact, they can be tamed by feeding them bones, turning them into allies. Wild wolves will attack livestock unprovoked, however, and thus can be a danger if you are trying to raise cows, pigs, or sheep.

10

SLIME

- **HEALTH:** 16 (large), 4 (small), 1 (tiny)

- **EXP:** 4 (large), 2 (small), 1 (tiny)

- **ENCOUNTERED:** In swamp biomes and underground.

- **SPECIAL ABILITIES:** Slimes come in three sizes. Large slimes split into two medium slimes when destroyed, and medium slimes split into two small slimes. You can also prevent them from spawning by manipulating the environment.

- **WEAKNESSES:** Slimes will always follow the shortest path to the player, and they can drown, so lure them off a cliff or into a body of water. If you have to fight them the old-fashioned way, kill off smaller slimes before splitting up bigger ones or you might get overwhelmed. Small slimes deal no damage, but they can push you around.

11

MAGMA CUBE

- **HEALTH:** 16 (large), 4 (small), 1 (tiny)

- **EXP:** 4 (large), 2 (small), 1 (tiny)

- **ENCOUNTERED:** Mercifully, only in the Nether.

- **SPECIAL ABILITIES:** The magma cube is the slime from hell. They come in multiple sizes, like slimes, and the bigger ones split into two smaller ones when destroyed. To make it worse, they're also immune to fire.

- **WEAKNESSES:** None, really. Sniping with a bow from safely beyond their jumping range, or a custom-made bunker, is probably the best way to go. Follow our advice for slimes, picking off the smallest pieces first.

12

GHAST

- **HEALTH:** 10 ⊪ **EXP:** 5

- **ENCOUNTERED:** Only in the Nether.

- **SPECIAL ABILITIES:** Ghasts are giant, flying ghost squids with a ton of health that shoot exploding fireballs at you. These not only deal damage, but can destroy the terrain around you.

- **WEAKNESSES:** Due to the terrain of the Nether, it's unlikely you'll ever get to attack one of these fiends up close, and using a bow requires you to put yourself in the line of fire for its attacks. Cover is useless, since Ghasts can just blow it up. Your best bet is speed: take a shot and then get out of the way before its explosive fireball lands. Use speed potions.

ENCHANTMENTS GUIDE

HARNESS ANCIENT powers to create marginally stronger shovels! Enchanting is one of the final skills to master before you can call yourself a true Minecraft expert. Here's how:

THESE PAGES HAVE ENCHANTED ME!

1 POWER UP

THE MAXIMUM level cost for enchantments is 30, but on its own the enchantment table can only perform Level 8 upgrades. To enhance it you need 15 bookshelves, positioned around the table – just like we have created in the screenshot above.

2 LUCK OF THE DRAW

DROP A weapon or armour in an enchanting table and you'll be given three random options to choose from. Each enchantment costs levels, which are earned from XP orbs dropped when you kill a monster. Higher level enchantments cost more levels.

3 LEVEL CURVE

THE HIGHER your level, the more XP it takes to level up. So if you're level 40 and buy two level 20 enchantments, one of them has cost much more XP than the other. To enchant efficiently, try taking something to the table every time you hit level 30.

4 EXAMPLE ENCHANTMENTS

WEAPON ENCHANTMENTS are fairly straightforward, with many of them increasing damage per level against specific enemy types: Smite for undead, Bane of Arthropods for spiders, and Sharpness for a smaller, universal boost. You may also come across a Looting enchant, increasing the drop rate of such rare materials such as Blaze Powder and Wither Skulls.

Tool enchants are some of the most useful in the game. Silk Touch allows you to harvest blocks that would normally be destroyed or broken down into components when demolished.

Efficiency increases the speed with which you mine, chop or dig. Unbreaking can greatly extend the life of your tools, by reducing the chance that each strike will damage their durability.

5 BY YOUR POWERS COMBINED...

UNLIKE POTION effects, you don't necessarily have to settle for just one enchantment on an item. It's possible to get two by using an anvil. When two items of different types are placed on an anvil, combining them will create an item with both enchantments. Not all combinations are allowed, however, and you will have to pay an experience cost to create the combined enchantment.

6 ON THE BOOKS

IT'S ALSO possible to store enchantments in books, to apply to an item later, trade to a friend or just for the satisfaction of carrying a bunch of enchanted books around like the boss wizard you are. You may also come across enchanted books in dungeon chests, around strongholds and temples.

KNOW YOUR BIOMES
BADLANDS

INCREDIBLY RARE, BADLANDS biomes (originally called Mesa) are home to red sand, hardened clay and stained clay blocks. Stained clay blocks are available in the same 16 colours as wool blocks, so make a great alternative building material. If you manage to find the even rarer Eroded Badlands biome then you'll be treated to expansive views of hardened clay spires. These structures are inspired by the real life Bryce Canyon, in Utah, USA.

DYED CLAY IS A MORE RESISTANT AND RELIABLE CRAFTING MATERIAL THAN DYED WOOL. ALSO, IT WON'T SET FIRE WHEN STRUCK BY LIGHTNING.

THOUGH THE STAINED CLAY SPAWNING NATURALLY IN THE BADLANDS COMES IN 16 COLOURS, YOU'LL HAVE TO GATHER SOME HARDENED CLAY TO DYE YOURSELF SHOULD YOU WANT TO GET A SPECIFIC COLOUR COMBO.

THE BADLANDS BIOME IS, IN MANY WAYS, QUITE SIMILAR TO THE DESERT BIOME. OF COURSE, THIS BLUE STUFF ISN'T HELPING US TO REINFORCE THAT CLAIM, IS IT NOW?

PUZZLES

Test your brain with these teasers...

I ALWAYS HAVE A BLAST WITH WORDSEARCHES!

ANSWERS ON PAGE 93

CREEPER SEARCH

HOW EXPLOSIVE are your word finding skills? Hidden inside this Creeper head are **15 Minecraft mob names!** They can be down, across or diagonal. Happy searching!

T	U	R	T	L	E	V	E	X	P
Z	N	I	P	I	G	C	K	D	O
O	S			A	R			O	L
M	L			B	N			L	I
B	I	P	O			D	E	P	R
I	M	A				A	H	R	B
E	E	R				R	I	E	E
T	C	R		S	T		C	N	I
E	F	O	X	H	U	S	K	O	R
B	A	T	D	S	H	E	E	P	W

DINNER TIME!

IT'S DINNER time in the world of Minecraft, and these happy Mobs are all chomping down on something new. Can you **follow the lines** to work out which animal is eating which food? Anything left over, you can scoff yourself!

YUM... ARE THERE ANY FLIES FOR ME?

CREEPER CHRISTMAS CRACKER!

Just a little bit louder than your average cracker, and no joke!

40 MINUTES!

START HERE!

1 WHEN THIS baby explodes, you're going to want some *seeerious* space between you and it. It's best to operate in a vast expanse of flat snow plains, if you can locate one: this gives you the room to build a Christmas Cracker as big as you'd like, and naturally flat ground means that you don't have to charge around for hours with your shovel. Bonus points if you manage a festive backdrop of spruce trees!

DIFFICULTY

HARD
LOTS OF TRICKY BLOCKS TO LAY IN THIS BUILD

2 PLACE TWO blocks of TNT next to each other. Take a few steps back. And then a few more. Just to be safe. Next, take some redstone dust and start laying out fuses at either end of the TNT. Ensure that there are no breaks in your simple redstone circuits, or your giant cracker might go out with a fizzle instead of a bang. Two fuses, one at each end of your cracker, gives you the opportunity to invite a friend over to pull the other end.

3 IT'S A Creeper Christmas Cracker, so it's got to be sporting the colours of Team Obliterate-Everything-You-Love. Green, lime and light grey wool will help you create the look of Minecraft's most infamous mob. Start laying down the basic shape of the middle of the cracker (a kind of long tube) around the TNT. Don't worry about putting the wool in an exact colour order – just make sure you use plenty of each to simulate that multi-tonal, pixelated creeper-green.

4 CONTINUE TO build up and over your TNT. You're going for a design that looks like the cracker is half-buried in the snow, so a long tunnel shape works well. As you build, take care not to block or interrupt your redstone fuses in any way, or your cracker won't explode, and you'll have to start all over again. Top tip: WATCH OUT FOR CREEPERS. It'd be painfully ironic if one of those pig-abominations blew up your tribute to his sneaky brother.

WHO IS CALLING ME CRACKERS? I'LL GET YOU!

5 CRACKERS ARE tied at each end, so you'll be needing some ribbons on your exploding surprise. Any colour wool will look fine (feel free to experiment), but red is very Christmassy put next to creeper-green. The ribbon's shape can be a bit fiddly to lay out though, so looking at some pictures might help at this point. Take heart in the knowledge that your creeper cracker is going to look positively adorable with a big red bow on his head.

6 WHAT ARE the end bits of Christmas crackers called? Handles? Arms? Wings? Who knows. Anyway, it's those parts that you now need to design. Have them taper out from the centre of your ribbons, which should look like they're pinching the cracker in. Extend them out so they equal the width of the centre tube. Looking good! Only one more detail to add to complete your cracker...

7 IT DOESN'T matter how many shades of emerald he is, or even whether he has all four of his stumpy legs: a creeper simply isn't a creeper without his perturbed expression. Take some black wool and slap two eyes and a sad little mouth smack-dab in the middle of your cracker. In case that nasty mug isn't already burnt into your retinas after years of dungeon encounters, use a creeper head as a reference. Ta-dah! Now that's the face of something about to get blown sky-high.

BUILD THIS!

8 GRAB A friend, a redstone torch, and a camera – it's time to light it up. Count to three, and then stick your torches at each end of the circuit. BOOM! That hidden TNT will cause your Creeper Christmas Cracker to do what creepers do best: detonate in a burst of rage and gunpowder. Cool. As for a prize, maybe you'll uncover some coal. If you're lucky, maybe you'll find a hidden cave system with tons of loot in your crater!

Make it!
CREEPER PIÑATA

CREEPER PIÑATA

INFO

TIME NEEDED: 30 MINUTES
EXTRA INFO: THIS IS THE PERFECT MINECRAFT MAKE FOR A BIRTHDAY PARTY!

YOU'LL NEED...

INGREDIENTS: Cardboard box, green crepe paper, black paper, PVA glue or double-sided sticky tape, yarn, sweets, sellotape, wooden skewer, scissors

BOXY!

USING THE point of your scissors (being careful with sharp points!), make a small hole in the middle of your box's top side. (You might find it hard to source a cube-shaped box for this, so it's fine to use a rectangular one. If you desperately want a cube for accuracy, you could make your own out of cardboard, but it won't be as sturdy.) Fold a length of yarn into a loop and tie a large, strong knot in the end, then thread the loop through the hole in the box so that the knot remains on the inside. Use sellotape to secure it. You always wondered what was inside a Creeper, right?

1 CREEPY!

YOU CERTAINLY wouldn't be alone if you'd ever thought that the best way to sort out a Creeper would be to give him a sharp clip around the ear. Problem is, in-game that tends to leave you with a destroyed house, if you aren't careful. This Creeper piñata, though, will explode in a shower of goodies, leaving you with a floor covered in sweets. Don't know about you, but we'd definitely prefer that to the other option...

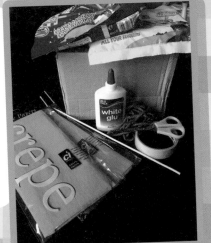

POKING HOLES

WITH YOUR wooden skewer, poke lots of little holes all over the sides and bottom of your box. This might sound like a silly thing to do, but it means that your piñata is more likely to break open once you start hitting it – if your cardboard is quite thick, it's definitely worth giving it a bit of help so that you're not bashing away at it forever!

WARNING

ASK MUM, DAD, OR WHOEVER LOOKS AFTER YOU TO HELP WITH SHARP SCISSORS!

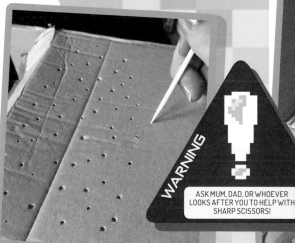

CREPE-ING AROUND!

COVER YOUR box in green crepe paper, attaching it to the box using either PVA glue or double-sided sticky tape (whichever you'd prefer). If you use glue, though, you'll be able to see a slightly darker mottled effect where it's dried, which adds to the authentic Creeper look. You might want to use a few layers of crepe paper, especially if your box has labels on it that might show through otherwise. Once you're happy with it, leave it somewhere safe to dry completely – if you've used glue, it's worth leaving it at least overnight.

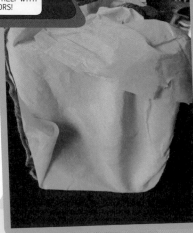

5 EYE EYE!

ONCE YOUR piñata is dry, cut out eyes and a mouth for your Creeper out of black paper. Attach them to the front of your box, ideally using double-sided sticky tape. Press them on really firmly.

> I ONCE WENT TO A PARTY – I HAD A REAL BLAST!

6 BOTTOMS UP!

CUT FOUR strips of crepe paper, and scrunch each one together at one end. Sellotape one of these to each corner of the bottom of your piñata – they'll dangle once it's hung up to give your Creeper its set of legs.

Why not make some miniature Creeper decorations to hang around your piñata for added effect? Simply follow the same steps outlined for the piñata itself – without the sweets, unless you're feeling incredibly destructive and want to smash everything in sight – using smaller boxes to create a whole family of dastardly decorations. Just look around the kitchen for inspiration: stock-cube boxes, egg boxes and so on would all work. If you prefer, you could also fill these with sweets to use instead of party bags – Creepers for everyone!

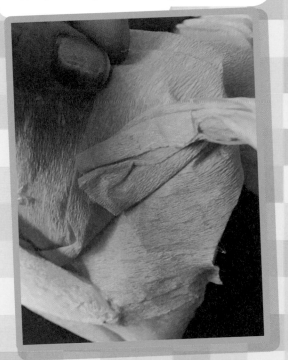

7 PARTY TIME!

WHEN IT'S party time, fill your Creeper with all kinds of sweets, hang up your piñata, fetch a stick and set to destroying it! Thankfully, this is one Creeper who won't cause any damage when he explodes – unless you count the damage to your teeth from the sugar in all those sweets, that is...

A-Z OF MINECRAFT

Going back to school with the ABCs of Minecraft...

A

IS FOR... APPLE

A IS always for apple in alphabets, isn't it? Well, the humble fruit isn't so basic in the world of Minecraft. Sure, it's the first food you'll find, but its mystical powers don't stop at "can be shoved into your pie-hole to restore four food points". They're also a great way to bribe horses into giving free rides, the key to making the super-secret Mojang banner, and like everything, extra-delectable when dipped in obscene amounts of gold.

What's more, Golden Apples are a reference to Greek myths involving blingin' apples that granted immortality (we'd prefer Immortality Pizza, if it's all the same). Munching one down triggers enhanced health regeneration for five precious seconds, with Enchanted Golden Apples dishing out 20 seconds of regen plus absorption. Also, you won't get scurvy! Always a bonus, right?

AND ALSO FOR... ALPHA

LOOKING AT Minecraft now, it's hard to believe that it was once just an ickle baby, equal parts bugs and promise. Unbelievably, the first-ever version of the game took a mere six days to make. Notch began work on Alpha Minecraft on May 10, 2009, working until May 16 to get it spick and span for its public release the very next day. There was just one mode – Survival – and Notch would frequently post "Seecret Updates" on Twitter announcing or confirming major changes to the game, like minecarts, redstone and sneaking. Simpler times. If you're getting all misty-eyed thinking about those long-forgotten days, never fear: you can still play ye olde Minecraft through the in-game launcher.

B IS FOR... BLOCK

BIOMES, BUCKETS and blazes are all very well, but blocks are literally the stuff that Minecraft's made of. When Notch's procedurally-generated universe rocked up in 2009, its cuboid charms appealed to us graphically-spoilt gamers. Other games sweated over making hyper-realistic worlds; Minecraft gave us square pumpkins, put on a sweet pair of shades and told us to deal with it.

Those blocks make reminiscing about epic Minecraft adventures a bit mind-boggling. One block is equal to one IRL cubic metre – meaning each in-game world is bigger than some planets. Go ahead and scrape the remainders of your mind off the wall. Done? Here's a different kind of block fact: update 1.9 adds craftable shields into Minecraft to let you block mob melee and projectile attacks.

C IS FOR... CREATIVITY

THERE'S ONLY one thing about Minecraft beginning with the letter C that's worth mentioning. That'd be creativity of course, and definitely nothing horrible, green and explody, perish the thought. Minecraft's free-roaming, resource-stuffed Creative Mode has prompted works of art: impossibly-detailed reconstructions of the Game of Thrones fantasy continent of Westeros; working 16-bit computers; a playable guitar; the entire country of Denmark; that 200-block-high portrait of your cat (still not judging, we promise). Thanks to Creative Mode's infinite possibilities, if you can dream it in Minecraft, you can do it – meaning the game's used as an educational building tool in schools around the world. What 'C' could possibly be more important than the spirit of artistry that Minecraft inspires in all of us? NOTHING... Oh God, it's right behind me, isn't i- *CREEPER EXPLOSION*

D IS FOR... DIAMONDS

AHH, DIAMONDS. Light of our lives, fire of our torches, object of all our late-night mining sessions (just five more minutes... honest). Why do we players worship them so fervently? Is it because they make the strongest, most efficient gear? Perhaps. Is it because crafting an Enchantment Table is impossible without them? Probably. Is it because we want to build ourselves a throne made entirely of blocks of diamond and force our friends to bring us cake as we sit in it? Ding ding ding! Our survey says: undoubtedly! A tough dream to realise, as diamond is the second rarest item in the game behind emerald – but strip-mining around the tenth or eleventh layer next to lava increases the likelihood of treasure-hunting triumph. Gimme that bling!

E
IS FOR... ERROR

YOU CAN'T have Minecraft without failure. It's an essential characteristic of the game. In fact, if you're not regularly failing at Minecraft, you're doing it wrong. Every grisly death, misplaced pickaxe, wasted resource and accidental base bonfire is a step in the right direction. All the best Minecraft stuff comes from mistakes. The iconic creeper itself was a coding error: Notch attempted to make a pig and mixed up the X and Y coordinates. The awesomely creepy Enderman sounds are actually warped English words like "hiya", "what's up?", and "this way" played in reverse. The $2.5 billion behemoth game itself was even born of failure: Notch never finished high school, coding the sensation we know and love while living in his mother's basement. Error equals WinRAR with Minecraft.

F
IS FOR... FRIENDS

THERE'S MANY a thrill to be had playing Minecraft in single player mode. It's all kinds of fun to tell anyone who'll listen the harrowing tale of that one time you were all alone, backed up against the dungeon wall, fending off three – no, five! – angry zombies with just a pork chop and your wits to call on. But multiplayer Minecraft on the game's servers is even better. Whether it's surviving the Nether together with friends, or constructing an elaborate free-running map to race for the title of Master Of Hardcore Parkour, a little company goes a long way when you're off in search of fame and the Farlands. And if you're the shy, retiring type and aren't too keen on real meat-based people? Dogs, ocelots, iron golems and snowmen make great in-game pals, defending you from mobs. Here boy, nice kitty...

G
IS FOR... GHAST

MINECRAFT'S MOST weird and wonderful mob just had to have its very own place in our A-to-Z (because it threatened to fireball us into crispy oblivion if it didn't.) There's so much to know and love – well, tolerate – about the demon jellyfish ghost. Oh, you thought the Ender Dragon was king of the mobs? Pshhh. Ghasts are even bigger by volume – the biggest baddie in the whole game. Their childlike gurgling/cooing/screaming is shudder-inducing: there's actually an unused sound file in the game's code called affectionate_scream.ogg. We'd be enchanted, if we weren't seriously disturbed. That auditory horror is based on a recording of the Minecraft music producer's sleepy cat, apparently. Aww? Stock up on cobblestone before you head off to the Nether to meet a ghast: it's the only block they can't destroy.

H
IS FOR... HEART

DON'T GET too excited, okay? We just see you as a friend. The heart symbol is a complex signifier in Minecraft, meaning many important things when it pops up around your UI. Breeding your cows, sheep and chickens will result in a scarlet flurry of happy little hearts bobbing around, indicating that you'll soon be hearing the pitter-patter of tiny hooves or claws. Or whatever sheep have. It's also the shape of your health meter. Red hearts lined up like ducks in a row = good. Empty containers jumping around like they're bunny rabbits at a trampoline-carpeted rave = bad. They'll go all lovely and golden if you're under the effects of Absorption – and if you're playing on Hardcore difficulty? Check out those angry little eyes. Cute!

I IS FOR... INVENTORY

YOUR MINECRAFT inventory says a lot about you. Do you harbour a messy hodge-podge of trinkets you've accumulated on your blocky travels? You utter slob, you. Or a clinically-sterile, hyper-organised homage to mining efficiency? Congratulations – you're a serial killer! Stay away from us. We jest, we jest. But we spend so much time staring at those neat little rows of grey boxes that it's left a permanent gridded overlay on our vision. Taking inventory is such an essential Minecraft experience that you even get an achievement the first time you open it. Soon, it becomes your best friend: holding all your important tools and tidbits in its hotbar; waiting patiently as you eject all and sundry to make room for new loot; offering you life advice and cups of tea during those difficult break-ups... Okay, so maybe not that last one, but it's still pretty handy. You'll have to sort out the beverages yourself, mind.

J IS FOR... JUKEBOX

WHAT'S EVEN more fun than bopping zombies on the head? Why, bopping to a fire mixtape as you do so, of course! Enter the jukebox, Minecraft's resident quadratic DJ, with sick beatz for all and a heart of diamond. Yes, of diamond, not gold. Its jewel-centric crafting recipe is likely a reference to the diamond-tipped needles of Edison phonographs. The music discs it plays can be found in dungeons chests, or dropped in the happy (yet rare) event of a creeper getting skewered by a skeleton's arrow. All the tracks are composed by Minecraft music producer C418 – and the guy's so jive-crazy that his character skin has a jukebox for a head. Now that's commitment.

K IS FOR... KILLING

ALL TOGETHER now: *'it's the ciiiircle of liiiife'*... Murder is sort of a given in Minecraft's Survival mode. It's them or us, after all. At least the constant massacring is sort of humane, as conquered creepers and crawlers disappear in a puff of smoke, XP and loot. It's alright, Timmy, they've just gone to a nice farm somewhere.

The real kicker is when they get the best of you, though. There's nothing quite like dropping a full set of diamond tools down a dangerous ravine upon death – except maybe sick puppies and eating glass. At least the game's death messages have a sense of humour about it all: reading that your friend "tried to swim in lava" after they take a dive in a too-hot spring is always chuckle-worthy. And anyway, everything respawns in Minecraft! Take note, real life.

L IS FOR... LEGO

EVERYBODY'S FAVOURITE plastic stickybricks were most likely the unintentional inspiration behind Minecraft. Notch himself has a sneaking suspicion that his childhood stash of LEGO influenced him to create a blocky game about, well, creating. And we're just going to throw this out there: Minecraft is better than LEGO. Stay with us. There's no boring clean-up process, no accidentally-on-purpose-swallowed pieces (in our defence, those studs look remarkably like Skittles), and no soul-splintering agony induced by stepping on rogue bricks. Plus, Minecraft's got monsters to battle and integrated quests to complete – so we'll pass on your silly little dioramas, thanks. Hang on. Is that Minecraft LEGO over there? Mother of Ender Pearl, that's all our dreams come true! We take it all back.

M IS FOR... MODDING

THERE'S NOTHING wrong with good ol' fashioned vanilla. But if it's a choice between that and triple-fudge rocky road sprinkled with rainbows and drizzled in dreams, we know what we'd pick. This is a convoluted ice-cream analogy through which we're trying to explain that modding the vanilla game is one of the best parts of playing Minecraft. But all it's done is left us hungry and you a little confused. Forget the ice cream. Booting up mods via ModLoader or Forge totally changes your game. Sample thousands of new, exotic foodstuffs; explore hundreds of fantastical biomes; marvel at the majestic sight of an entire farm of exploding chickens. You can even alter or add in entire game mechanics. Mods are a bit complicated – but take care to back up those save files, proceed with caution, and you can keep Minecraft fresh forever. There's literally no excuse to stop playing! (Sorry, Mum).

N IS FOR... NOTCH

WELL, WELL, well. Look who's somehow sneaked into our alphabet. We're kidding, Notch! Please don't patch us out! Markus 'Notch' Persson is the man who created Minecraft, and he actually started making videogames from the tender age of eight. It may not surprise you, then, to learn that the loveable, fedora-clad meatball is actually a part of the Swedish branch of Mensa. (The gang for smart folk). Mojang's founder is no longer involved in Minecraft matters *sob* after he sold it to tech giant Microsoft for mad cash. Why would he be, when he could be chilling out at his $70 million pad next to his M&M-DISPENSING WALL? Yep, that's a real thing. And that mysterious moniker? Well, it means... absolutely zilch. He picked it because it sounded cool, apparently.

O IS FOR... OCEAN

ENDLESS AND imposing, the cavernous depths of the game's procedurally-generated worlds hide the most unbelievable secrets. The blue biome is an infinite source of delicious sashimi for those savvy enough to rustle up a fishing rod, and zipping around its azure surface in a wooden boat is a pleasant diversion.

But beware, all ye landlubbers: what lies beneath is far more chilling than you could possibly imagine. Here be dangerous ocean monuments guarded by, er, guardians, as it happens. The strange, spiky cyclops-fish has a death-stare that'll fire a laser at you as soon as look at you. Gulp. Just think of the awesome rewards! Whole blocks of gold – and sponges! You'll never want for a dishcloth again: definitely worth the risk of drowning.

P IS FOR... PIG

BEHOLD, THE golden rule of Minecraft (and of life): when in doubt, bacon. Just the goofy expressions on the faces of these pixelated porkers can get you through the hard times. When a creeper lays waste to the labour of love that was your redstone auto-farm, solace arrives in the form of some light-hearted piggybacking. A saddle, a stick, some string and a tasty carrot later, you've got yourself a regular rodeo.

Until you get peckish, of course. A heartbreaking coincidence, indeed, that your porcine pal also happens to be made of crackling. C'est la vie. At least the boss-eyed effigy of Minecraft's benign swine will live on eternally in the form of the adorable Reuben the pig, star of Telltale's Minecraft: Story Mode series.

Q IS FOR... QUIZ

HEADS UP off your desks, Minecraft scholars. We're quite a way into our alphabet here, so let's check you've been paying attention. Time for a pop quiz...

Q1: What S is a brand-new item that lets you block enemy attacks?

Q2: What C is a type of block that ghosts can't destroy?

Q3: What E speaks English backwards?

Q4: What D is the key ingredient in crafting a jukebox?

Q5: What G can be found in ocean monuments?

Turn in your test papers, please. What do you mean, prize? Your prize is a quiet sense of satisfaction and us not expelling you from Mineschool.

ANSWERS 1. Shield **2.** Cobblestone **3.** Enderman **4.** Diamond **5.** Guardian

R IS FOR... REDSTONE

SO YOU'VE just seen a player press a button and automatically farm a whole field of wheat like it ain't even a thing. Magic! Sorcery! Burn the witch! Calm down, it's just redstone. No-one could accuse Minecraft of being a simple game. It has its very own and surprisingly deep circuitry system built right in, and players have done amazing things with it. Epic minecart rollercoasters stretching on for miles, automatic machine guns that can farm and fire arrows... There's even a redstone mod called bitCraft that lets you work lights and alarms IRL by using in-game redstone communications. And if you can't quite wrap your head around all those repeaters, all you need to know is that mining the red stuff will net you mad XP.

S IS FOR... STEVE

HE'S A man of few words, our Steve – and by few, we mean none. Minecraft's silent protagonist stands 6'1" tall and is now shorn of his luxuriant beard (the one that looked like a goofy grin). But don't be fooled by his affable mug: the stats suggest that Steve's actually some sort of terrifying demi-god. Not only can he fly in Creative mode, his casual walking pace is a blistering 9.7mph. Good grief, Steven, don't you ever stop to smell the roses?

He's also capable of sporting a full set of golden armour, which would weigh roughly 2892kg. When he's not chilling out in two-ton duds, he's holding his breath underwater for a maximum of 15 seconds – and seeing as though the Minecraft day is only 20 minutes long, that's a real-world time of 18 minutes. We'll just back away slowly...

T IS FOR... TORCH

WE NEVER thought we'd be the sort of people to cuddle inanimate, virtual objects while crying, but Minecraft's wonderful torches have saved our custom skins on more than several occasions.

You're never alone with a torch. Got lost on a jaunt away from your base and now the inky darkness of night-time is upon you? Torch. Mobs spawning on your roof and plopping down your chimney like unseasonable Santa Clauses? Torch. Exploring the ocean floor and swiftly running out of that oxygen nonsense you so desperately need to live? Potion of Water Breathing. Only joking, that stuff's expensive. TORCH. There is only the torch. Yep, the humble fiery tool can even be used to create temporary air pockets underwater, when used correctly. As soon as torch/human marriage is legal, we'll be straight down the registry office. Did we just write that out loud? Ahem...

U IS FOR... UNDERGROUND

MUCH LIKE the Seattle music scene, most of Minecraft is underground. You can go several Minecraft days, if not weeks without seeing the light of day – and that's just how we like it. Each randomly generated cavern branching off into winding tunnels must be combed for exposed ore; each lava lake doused in our efforts to mine obsidian; each ravine explored for an entrance to abandoned mineshafts. You're certainly not going to get to The End without hours of world excavation, as strongholds house end portals (and silverfish, but we try not to think about those. Ugh.) Cheerio, sunlight. Vitamin D be damned: it's all about Vitamin DIAMOND.

V IS FOR... VISTAS

IT'S ALL too easy to get caught up in the busywork of Minecraft and miss out on the little things. It's astonishing that a world composed entirely of 1x1 blocks can randomly generate such sublime horizons. Each corner you round can confront you with new landmarks.

Struggling to find a picturesque rambling location? A quick Google search will provide you with world seeds famed for their natural beauty – simply copy and paste the number into the corresponding field when creating a world, and voila! Forget building your house in a structurally-sound location: really, you just want a view of those floating falls when you're drinking your morning coffee/Health Potion. Load up some fancy shaders, apply a gorgeous texture pack, and build those glass windows high...

W IS FOR... WEATHER

WE'RE A British book, so of course we're going to talk your ear off about the weather in Minecraft. The forecast's clear and sunny by default (if only we could extract the code for this from the game's files), and you can toggle rain and snow on and off with a simple "/weather rain" command, which would certainly come in handy in real life. Easier than a brolly, too.

But things really kick off when it gets stormy. Thunderstorms are preceded by a darkness so complete that you're able to sleep in a bed during it. The lightning's the worst bit: everything it strikes, it sets on fire... including you, to the tune of five hearts of damage. A short, sharp shock hurts us, but gives certain mobs superpowers – how is that fair, Notch?! Zapped pigs turn into zombie pigmen, villagers into witches, and creepers into glowing blue charged creepers. Oh well – we were indoors people, anyway. Might brighten up later.

X

IS FOR... X MARKS THE SPOT

SQUASH TOGETHER a compass and a few sheets of paper, and you've got yourself a map that'll update in real-time as you explore your individually-generated Minecraft world. But what good is a map without a lovely, fat, juicy X to encourage you to hunt something shiny? If you've got a predilection for piracy, searching for treasure with your pals is a brilliant way to raise the stakes. Thanks to downloadable maps and server plug-ins, it's possible to decipher and follow player-made clues to find hoards of jewels and gold hidden in them there hills. Pack a sword, some steaks and grab your mates for the epic adventure ahead, but don't be too discouraged if the plunder proves elusive – the greatest treasure you'll find is friendship. D'awww.

Y

IS FOR... YOUTUBE

ONE THING'S for sure: Minecraft would not be the worldwide phenomenon it is today without the power of the Internet, and specifically video-hosting website YouTube. Don't believe us? Well, get a load of this actual science we dug up: a doctoral student at the Annenberg School of Communication conducted a study that showed one third of early Minecraft players discovered the game through YouTube videos.

Stampylonghead, Sky, CaptainSparkles, iBallisticSquid, iHasCupcake... No, we're not spouting nonsense – these are just some of the usernames of the YouTubers who've shown the world, with their own unique brands of yelling and #YOLO'ing, why Minecraft is so much fun. And Minecraft has honoured them. In one console version of the game, you could find an obsidian-based, four-gold-block high Tower of Pimps: a reference to popular YouTube channel Achievement Hunter.

Z

IS FOR... ZOMBIE

FINALLY, BRINGING up the rear as usual, shambles in the Minecraft zombie. The reason you never see a zombie in a stylish pair of specs? They've got the best eyesight in the game. They'll spot you from 40 blocks away, compared to other mobs squinting at your wobbly knees from just 16 blocks. They can still accessorise, though, occasionally sporting a fetching pumpkin hat or even diamond armour. The

Rotten Flesh that they drop on death is as gross as it is useless, but we love 'em anyway. Seeing a baby zombie speed around on a chicken is a magical Minecraft moment. So let's celebrate the green guy: spawn a giant one into your world with the command / summon Giant.

KNOW YOUR BIOMES
MUSHROOM FIELDS

IT'S NOT JUST the prospect of shroomy soup to cook up that makes the discovery of a mushroom fields biome a good thing. Hostile mobs won't spawn here, even underground or at night, so this is an ideal place to build a base. You will need to bring your own livestock and seeds for farming, though. Mushroom biomes are always found near the ocean, often as isolated islands. Build a big home and invite friends to become a real fun guy...

USE AN AXE TO TAKE DOWN THESE BIG 'SHROOMS. DON'T FORGET TO REPLANT ANY HARVESTED MUSHROOMS. YOU CAN USE BONE MEAL TO GROW THEM BIG AGAIN.

BEFORE YOU START SHEARING MOOSHROOMS FOR THEIR RED MUSHROOMS, REMEMBER THAT ONCE THEY'VE BEEN SHORN THEY'LL TURN INTO REGULAR OLD COWS. BETTER TO MILK THEM (USING A BOWL) TO GET MUSHROOM STEW!

MYCELIUM GROWS ON DIRT LIKE GRASS, BUT IS BETTER FOR GROWING MUSHROOMS. YOU CAN'T USE THIS STUFF FOR FARMING NORMALLY, SO BRING SOME DIRT BLOCKS WITH YOU FOR A BASE.

PUZZLES
Test your brain with these teasers...

WE'VE FILLED IN A FEW LETTERS FOR YOU!

NAME THAT MOB

TIME TO test your knowledge of mobs, can you name them from a quick look at their faces? Try your luck with these nasty beasties...

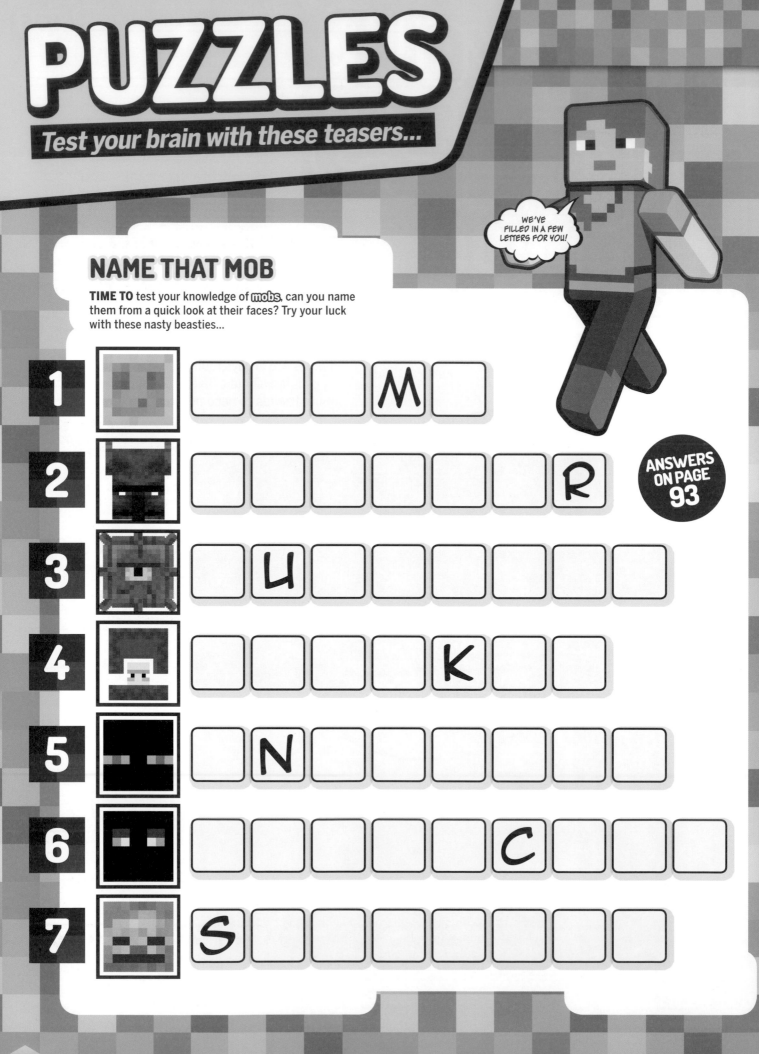

1 ☐ ☐ ☐ M ☐

2 ☐ ☐ ☐ ☐ ☐ ☐ R

ANSWERS ON PAGE **93**

3 ☐ U ☐ ☐ ☐ ☐ ☐ ☐

4 ☐ ☐ ☐ ☐ K ☐ ☐

5 ☐ N ☐ ☐ ☐ ☐ ☐

6 ☐ ☐ ☐ ☐ C ☐ ☐ ☐

7 S ☐ ☐ ☐ ☐ ☐ ☐

LIGHTNING CODE

THUNDERSTORMS CAN happen at any time in the **Overworld**, and the **lightning** is responsible for turning **Pigs** into **Zombie Pigmen** and making **Creepers super charged**! This lightning bolt hides a **secret code** – follow the bolt of lightning and trace the pattern on the letter block to discover what it says!

M	G	R	C	W
I	L	F	N	T
X	N	E	L	F
W	C	F	C	P
A	C	R	R	L
S	N	A	I	C
K	F	R	O	B
E	R	T	W	T
S	W	A	S	A
S	A	T	S	C
J	A	M	R	X
D	S	T	E	P
H	E	L	F	C
M	Q	B	4	W
D	T	U	N	I
D	C	O	H	F
G	T	F	C	L
H	C	I	P	K
V	S	H	M	F

Make it!
ENDERMAN CARD

YOU'LL NEVER MAKE ME!

INFO

ENDERMAN CARD

TIME NEEDED: 15 MINUTES
EXTRA INFO: YOU CAN TRY THIS WITH ALL KINDS OF MONSTERS AS POP UPS!

YOU'LL NEED...

INGREDIENTS: 2 sheets of purple card, 1 sheet of black paper, scrap paper, double-sided sticky tape, scissors, ruler, purple and silver sparkly gel pens

DIFFICULTY

EASY
MAKE SURE YOU HAVE SOME SAFE SCISSORS THOUGH!

1 SQUASHED TOMATOES

IT'S NEVER pleasant to look up and suddenly see the spindly limbs and glowing eyes of an Enderman towering over you. But what if, rather than trying to make you dead, he was actually just trying to wish you a happy birthday? There's only one way to find out: by making this pop-up card, and use it to surprise unsuspecting friends or family. Heck, at least this way they're fine to look him in the eye.

2 MAKE A CARD

FIRST THINGS first: you need to make your basic card that the pop-out will, well, pop out from. Take a piece of purple card that's twice the size you want your finished card to be, and fold it in half. We used a sheet of A4 card for this, but you could go as big or as small as you like. You want the fold to be nice and precise, so go over it a few times with your thumbnail.

4 MAKE GUIDES

OPEN UP your card base, and make two small pen marks – each 3cm from the central fold – roughly in the middle of the card's height. They're only for reference, and will soon be covered up, so make sure you keep them nice and small. This is the guide for your pop-up, so make sure they're even!

3 HOW BIG?

FROM YOUR other sheet of purple card, measure and cut out a rectangle 5cm long and 1cm wide (this is assuming you used an A4 piece of card – you'll need to make it a bit longer/shorter for a bigger/smaller card). Fold this rectangle in half, and fold each end towards the middle, about 1cm from the edge.

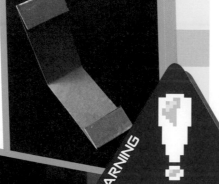

WARNING

ASK MUM, DAD, OR WHOEVER LOOKS AFTER YOU TO HELP WITH SHARP SCISSORS!

5 MAKING FEET

THE LITTLE tabs on your card rectangle will act as 'feet' for your pop-up – the small piece of card will act like a small hinge that stands up when you open the card. Cut two pieces of double-sided sticky tape that are the same size as these feet, and use them to attach your hinge to the card – stick each foot to one of the guide marks you made earlier. To make sure these stick really well, it's worth closing your card and placing some heavy books on top of it while you carry on with the next couple of steps.

6 DRAW IT!

USING SOME scrap paper, sketch out your Enderman figure, and then cut it out. You don't want him to be any taller or wider than your card – in fact, you want him just to pop out of the middle – so keep that in mind while you're drawing. As he's such a prominent feature of your card, it's also a good idea to fold your scrap paper in half, and sketch out just half of the figure against the fold – that way he'll be perfectly symmetrical when you cut him out. Don't worry if you're not great at drawing – this is just a template, and you can take as many tries as you need!

7 FOLD IT!

ONCE YOU'VE got an Enderman template that you're happy with, use it as a guide to carefully cut out your Enderman figure from your black paper. He'll need to have a fold going down his middle, so – as you did with your sketch – it will probably help to fold your black paper in half. Once you've done that, use your gel pens to give him his chilling, characteristic eyes.

8 TAPE IT!

SALVAGE YOUR card from under those books, and open it up. Put a strip of double-sided tape across the back of your Enderman (roughly where his belly button would be, if creepy, antisocial supernatural beings had such things), and then use this to attach him to your cardboard hinge. Make sure you line up the folds neatly!

9 WRITE IT!

WRITE IN a birthday message (or any other occasion) and your pop-up card is ready to pop! How you decorate the front is up to you – may we suggest a nice, clear, friendly Minecraft landscape to lure the recipient into a false sense of security...?

10 BEST PETS IN MINECRAFT!

Ordinary, exotic or extremely dangerous – why not try taming these ten incredible Minecraft pets?

IT CAN be a lonely existence playing Minecraft. Whether you're building a glorious palace for yourself or just pottering about having a splendid adventure, it's always nicer to have other people with you. But when your friends aren't around or your internet connection isn't working, you don't have to ditch the pickaxe – get yourself a pet, and you'll never be alone again!

You can share your adventures with Tweety, Fluffy or Mr Wuffles, or you can just keep them at home so you can come back each night and impress them with all the weird stuff you got up to during the day. The only thing about Minecraft is that technically there are only a limited amount of animals you can keep as 'pets', but we're choosing to bend the definition slightly (okay, a lot) and accept that all caged or captured animals count.

That means that we can have all the standard pig, chicken and ocelot pets, but we can also adopt adorable, vicious creatures that would kill us if they got the chance. Yay variety!

PIG

IN MINECRAFT, the humble pig is one of the easier animals to tame and domesticate, making him a great choice for the beginner who wants a little bit of oinky company.

Firstly, lure your potential piggy pal into an enclosed area with some carrots – this is where you'll be keeping him, so you can stick to the basics and build a little fenced-off pen, or you could go dramatic and build him a tiny pig-house.

Once he's in the pen/pig-house, close it off so he can't escape, and there you go! Your very own piggy friend. Put up a little sign with his name on if you like, grab him a girlfriend and breed your very own family of pigs, or get a saddle and a carrot on a stick and use him as a stylish (if a bit stinky) ride.

Or, alternatively, take a page out of the crazy minded Minecraft community and build yourself an automatic bacon/breeding line, which rounds up all the adult pigs and sets them on fire while all the piglets fall through to the layer below, giving them an excellent view of their parents getting cooked to a delicious crisp above. Is it worth murdering pigs in front of their children for an endless supply of bacon? Yes, of course. That's not even a difficult question. It's bacon, people.

CHICKEN

SO NOW you have your own pigs, you're looking to expand, right? Time to start turning your pig-loving livestock collection into a proper farm with the addition of chickens.

Similar to pigs, you'll have to lure them into an enclosed area, this time with wheat seeds, then block them in. Unlike pigs, which only drop items when killed, chickens give you eggs every five to ten minutes. However, killing them gives you raw chicken, and killing them with fire gives you cooked chicken, and if you would much rather farm the birds for their meat than their eggs, then you're in (c)luck: it's possible to build an automatic factory line to turn chickens into dinner!

All you need is a fairly complicated setup involving redstone circuits, lava (to cook them), some glass (to watch them get cooked) and you're in business! We won't judge.

On a less meaty note. If you, like us, look at this picture of a Minecraft chicken and go, "that's a duck," then you're not alone. Did Minecraft boss Notch not know what a chicken looked like? Because that is most definitely a duck. The Pocket Edition calls them ducks, Notch himself made a joke about renaming them ducks, and one of the loading screen messages on the Console Edition asks: "Is it a chicken, or a duck?" Yeah, we say it's a duck. We prefer ducks, anyway. Duck.

WOLF

THEY MIGHT be fairly rare, and you might have to venture into the dark woods or the chilly tundra to find them, but a tamed wolf is the closest to man's best friend you'll find in Minecraft.

Grab yourself a few bones to tame a wild wolf – each one has a one in three chance of taming the little guy, so keep trying if it doesn't work first time – and once you succeed, your new friend will get an orange collar and sit down, looking at you all lovingly.

His tail will rise and fall depending on his health, and he'll follow you around like a devoted pet, even to the point of teleporting to your location if you roam too far.

What else can you do with your new, loyal partner? Take him with you on adventures as your bodyguard! Anything that injures you or that you attack becomes an immediate target for your furry friend, and because there's no limit to how many you can have, why not become that guy who roams around the land with a pack of ferocious wolves?

MOOSHROOM

YOU'VE GOT yourself some pigs and chickens and you're well on your way to starting a pretty decent farm. What else do farms need? Cows, probably. But you're bored of your garden-variety domesticated farmyard animals, so it's time to get a little more exciting.

A mooshroom is a sort of cross between a regular cow and a mushroom, and the less you know about why that happened, the better. They're dappled red and white, with huge growing fungi all over their backs.

Like regular cows, they can be milked with a bucket or killed to create leather and beef. However, shearing them will give you red mushrooms – although it will turn them into a regular cow if you do – and milking a mooshroom with a bowl instead of a bucket gives you mushroom stew, which is more than a little bit disturbing.

Now, you can't exactly keep these beautiful specimens in a regular pen, so why not build a fitting monument to their mushroominess and build them a pen topped with giant mushrooms? That's more like it.

OCELOT

WOLVES MAY be the dogs of the Minecraft world, but ocelots are the cats. In the wild, they appear as yellow and black-spotted cats, stalking chickens and scaring away creepers. They won't attack you, but they can sprint – so you'll have to be clever if you want to catch one.

As with other animals, you need to grab yourself a lure, which in this case is an uncooked fish, and wait until your target ocelot approaches you and looks at you. At this point, you need to stay VERY STILL, or else you'll scare him away. Once he's decided he likes you, he will turn from his wild cat colouring into a tabby, siamese or tuxedo-patterned cat, and follow you back home, purring happily.

As with wolves, they will teleport to be near to you, making them much friendlier than real cats, and they will sit on pretty much anything – beds, chests, other cats – making that object unusable.

Keep a few fish on hand, because they can be a bit stubborn, but they're definitely worth it to keep away the creepers.

HORSE

A MAN walks into a bar. The barkeeper asks, "why the long face?" The man replies, "because I don't have a horse," before ordering a big drink. Avoid this unfortunate situation by getting yourself mankind's finest mount: the lovely horse.

You'll find them roaming the plains and savannas alongside donkeys, in 35 different colours. You can get brown, dark brown, even darker brown, black, grey, white, plus all of the above with various types of spots – whereas donkeys just come in your factory-standard grey-brown. Sorry, donkeys.

Unfortunately, horses are a bit trickier to tame than the animals we've seen so far, requiring you to mount them over and over again until the horse no longer bucks you off. Feeding them various items, such as sugar, wheat, and golden apples, will increase your chances, and a golden apple will also make a horse enter breeding mode. It sounds like a lot of work, but remember that you can put armour on horses, making them easily the most stylish pet you can have (until the pig fashion mod comes out, fingers crossed).

SILVERFISH

THE BEST thing about having silverfish as pets is that they're so tiny, you can have loads and they take up hardly any space. The first thing to remember is that they aren't actual fish, so don't make the mistake of building them a big watery tank only to find them drowned in the morning.

You may recognise them from strongholds, where smashing a block that looks suspiciously like all the other stone blocks will spawn a wiggly little dude intent on destroying you. He'll also wake up all his wiggly buddies, so even though they only do half a heart damage, they're quite lethal in large numbers.

Rather than luring these guys, which will be a pain considering how wiggly and fast they are, the best plan is to create a nice cage for them first – on creative mode, place a silverfish spawn block inside where you want them to be, and destroy it.

Add to your collection whenever you feel like he's getting lonely. They're pretty much the Minecraft equivalent of sea monkeys, not least because of the slightly disappointing reality and the similarly misleading name.

ELDER GUARDIAN

IF FARMYARD animals bore you, hostile creatures make you yawn, and the thought of killer bunnies excites you about as much as an hour in a dentist's waiting room, then maybe you're ready for the ultimate challenge – turning the not-very-cute, completely mad elder guardian into your personal plaything.

It looks like a cross between a really gross fish and a sea mine, and it's about as dangerous as giving a wedgie to a bear. The secret to capturing this tricky beast is patience. Patience, invisibility potions, careful manoeuvering, sobbing, and more patience.

You'll need to be invisible so it doesn't see you and kill you, and you'll need loads of minecart tracks to push him towards his new priso... we mean home. It's also handy to have milk on hand, because your new pet has an irritating habit of giving you mining fatigue, which makes a tricky job even worse. Luckily, milk negates that fatigue. Not so bored of cows now, are you?

SPIDER

NOTHING IS more cuddly than an adorable spider, crawling all over your hands and face and into your mouth. No? Not a fan of spiders? Perhaps you'll still enjoy having them as pets, merely because a spider in a cage is a spider that's not in your mouth. As long as you can see him, therefore, the chances of accidentally eating him are significantly lowered.

You can't argue with that kind of logic. Your first step is seeking out the spiders. Unlike spiders in the real world, they can't be found in your bed or at the back of your bookcase. Instead, you'll find them scuttling about anywhere that's dark, like caves, but darkness also makes them hostile, so be careful.

Make sure it's nighttime, and try to lure the spider back to the little spider home you've made for him while making sure to remember that the horrid thing can climb walls. Once you've trapped him, make sure to close off the ceiling so he can't climb out, then fill the cage with lava, because spiders are the worst. Repeat until no more spiders exist.

ZOMBIE PIGMAN

NOW WE'RE getting really interesting. Who said all your pets had to be animals? Technically, the zombie pigman isn't really a human or an animal – he's a pigman, which makes him a bit of both, and therefore it's totally acceptable to keep him/ it as a pet.

Because Minecraft doesn't encourage the capture and keeping of monsters as pets, there's no real way to lure him like there is with the other animals – you'll just have to make him pursue you to his new prison.

Pigmen are created either in the Nether or when lightning strikes within four blocks of a pig, so unless you want to settle down in a nightmarish hell-portal, you'd better find yourself a pig and pray to Thor.

Once you've found yourself a zombie pigman – or even better, a baby zombie pigman – get him to chase you into your pre-prepared cage. Make sure not to use any wooden doors – they'll knock them down faster than you can say: *"Heeere's Johnny"*. Give them a roof so they don't burn up in the sunlight and say hello to your new, fairly hostile pet zombie pigman!

Isn't it cute the way he screams as his flesh falls off his bones? Awwww.

A GINGERBREAD HOUSE

Make yourself a homestead that's good enough to eat...

60 MINUTES!

DIFFICULTY

HARD
LOTS OF CHALLENGE FOR BIG BUILD FANS IN THIS ONE

START HERE!

1 IF YOUR gingerbread house is for life, and not just for Christmas, then you've got to make sure you pick a sweet spot (geddit?). Level yourself some ground near a pretty ice lake and lay down some foundations. Dark oak planks make a great floor, and look quite like chocolate – your feet will be feeling uncomfortably sticky in no time. Start building the walls in orange stained clay: you can make your house as small or as large as you like. Now you're gingerbready for action.

2 TO THE windows, to the walls! Now it's time to build the main structure of your house. It's important that the front and back walls match, so that your roof goes on nice and evenly. Well who would want a wonky roof? Next, use those blocky little fists of yours to punch out holes for windows and a door (or two doors. Or three doors, if you like. FOUR DOORS?! I'm calling the police). Hmmm, what to do with all those broken bits of biscuit? Tidy them into your face. Om nom nom.

3 HAVING A giant mutant spider crash your Christmas dinner is generally considered to be "a bit of a bother." A roof, then, will be an important addition to your new home. Build it up on either side following the shape of the front and back walls to create a triangular roof. Take a look at the front of the house: you'll notice that the roof doesn't extend all the way across the top, leaving a few block-shaped gaps. These will come in really handy in the next step...

4 THIS IS where your sugary home starts to come to life – and where you start to get peckish – as you 'ice' your gingerbread house. Remember those block-shaped gaps? Plonk some snow blocks in them to give your roof that neat, freshly-iced look. You can add extra stripes of 'icing' along the roof with snow layers. A chocolate bar door can be achieved by using a dark oak one, and put stained glass panes in your windows to mimic melted boiled sweets. Be careful you don't get tooth panes! Hah.

5 **YOU CAN** get pretty creative with the kinds of sweets that you decorate your gingerbread house with. Blocks of stained glass come in loads of colours and look like boiled sweets, so you could decorate your house with those for a cool effect. Slime blocks make brilliant gumdrops: just be careful not to let a plague of actual Slimes loose on your painstakingly-crafted crib, or you'll be running for the Extreme Hills.

6 **STEP INSIDE** the house for a moment. Mmmm, the smell of freshly-baked gingerbread... Stop that! Focus. Focus more. How can you make your pad as festive and cosy as possible? You'll certainly need a chest to put all your presents in. Some bunkbeds will make the difficult Christmas Eve sleep a bit easier (and there's so much more room for activities!) Lastly, there's just about room for a teeny-tiny Christmas tree. Well, technically, it's a Christmas fern, but it'll do. Just don't tell Santa.

7 **EVEN THOUGH** your delicious den is already looking good enough to eat, a few finishing touches outside will make you the envy of all your neighbours. Make a snow golem by stacking two snow blocks and one pumpkin on top – he'll come to life and potter about your garden, looking for mobs to shoo away. Leave a friendly sign to let Santa know that you're expecting him to stop by on the 25th. Finally, you'll want something decorating your doorway. A Christmas wreath, maybe? Nah – how about a creeper head?

8 **OF COURSE,** there are those of you who dream bigger. There are those of you who think the traditional gingerbread cottage is boring and twee. There are, indeed, a select few of you who would persuade Mr Claus to visit your home not with friendly signs, but by force. To you, I present the Gingerbread Fortress: the ultimate in foodstuff fortification. With a bit more orange stained clay and snow, you can whip up a candy castle in no time. Check out those cake parapets!

BUILD THIS!

Make it!
SPIDER CUPCAKES

YOU'LL NEED...

INGREDIENTS: 100g plain flour, 140g caster sugar, 20g cocoa powder, 1½ tsp baking powder, 120ml milk, one large egg, vanilla extract, 190g butter (take it out of the fridge about an hour before you start), 450g icing sugar, black food dye, red wine gums, licorice sticks, icing bag, plain dark-coloured cake cases, 12-hole muffin tin

1 MAKE WONKA PROUD

ONE OF the worst things about spiders – both in Minecraft and in real life – is their eight horrible legs. Eight! That's almost ten! We decided to turn this grim feature of their anatomy to our advantage, turning their icky appendages into tasty licorice sticks. Oh, and turning their bodies into delicious home-baked chocolate cupcakes. And their evil eyes into wine gums. Basically, if Willy Wonka turned into a zookeeper, we would be his favourite employees...

I KNOW AN OLD LADY WHO SWALLOWED MY FRIEND BRIAN!

2 MIXY MIXY!

SET YOUR oven to 170° (or 150° if you have a fan oven) and leave it to heat up while you're making your cake mix. Boring, but important, that. In a large bowl, mix together your flour, sugar, cocoa powder, baking powder and 40g of the butter, until it looks a bit like chocolatey grit. If you have a mixer, this stage will be much easier – but it's still possible to do it with a wooden spoon and some patience!

WARNING

ASK MUM, DAD, OR WHOEVER LOOKS AFTER YOU TO HELP WITH KITCHEN EQUIPMENT!

3 GET CRACKING!

CRACK IN your egg, add a small splash of vanilla essence and mix it together – then add the milk a little bit at a time. Don't worry if the batter you end up with seems runnier than a normal cake mix – you'll end up with lovely, light cupcakes this way.

4 BAKE OFF FUN!

PUT A cake case in each of your tin's holes, and then carefully divide your cake mix between the 12 cases. They won't be full right to the top, but this leaves them enough space to rise. Bake them for around 25 minutes – you can tell when they're done by popping a sharp knife into the middle of one of the cakes and seeing if it comes out clean. Let them cool completely before you ice them.

5 COLOUR FUN!

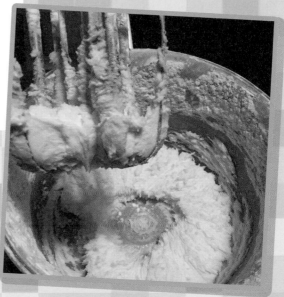

MIX THE remaining 150g of butter with the icing sugar until it forms a creamy icing – you might need to add a splash of milk or water to loosen it up a bit, but make sure you only put in a tiny bit at a time! Mix in your food dye until you get a deep black colour. Food dye tends to be stronger than food colouring, so start off slowly (and make sure you stick to the guidelines on the bottle for the maximum recommended amount).

6 ICING, ICING BABY!

FILL A disposable piping bag with your icing, and snip a V shape in the end – make it about 1cm across. Use the bag to pipe a thick swirl of icing on the top of each cake. Don't worry if it doesn't look perfect, as you'll be putting decorations on top as well!

7 SCARY FACES!

CUT YOUR red wine gums into small squares for eyes (you'll need two per cake, so 24 in total), and snip your licorice sticks into 'legs' a few centimetres long (eight legs per cake makes a whopping 96 of these). Arrange these various body parts on top of each cupcake, and enjoy your deliciously spooky handywork!

60 MINUTES!

THE LION, THE WITCH AND THE WARDROBE!

It's all gone a bit Narnia around here. Ooh, Turkish Delight...

START HERE!

1 PICK OUT the kind of Narnian woodland that you'd love to find at the back of a wardrobe. Cold Taiga biomes are especially perfect for this job, as they're snowy and thickly-forested. If you do manage to find a spot right in the middle of two biomes, then snap it up; the sudden transition into a winter wonderland will be even more magical. Simply knock up your standard wooden hut – or you could even start to build your enchanted wardrobe at the back of an existing build.

DIFFICULTY

MEDIUM
THE FINER DETAILS OF THIS BUILD ARE YOUR CHOICE

2 ONCE YOU'VE made a big hole in the wall (helpfully letting in all the snow) the exciting part can begin. Build the frame of the wardrobe around the hole, and pop a couple of doors on. You can now engineer the back of the wardrobe, which will essentially be a long corridor. Did I say corridor? Silly me! I meant magical portal that is definitely magic. If you hit trees as you go, build them into the structure to create the illusion of the wardrobe transforming into the forest.

THERE'S NOT MUCH ROOM IN THAT WARDROBE!

3 WOAH, WHERE do you think you're going?! It's not time to enter Narnia yet – we've still got furniture to assemble. Even a supernatural wardrobe needs clothes in it, so go back to the beginning of the corridor and put some wooden blocks on each wall. Coloured banners work well as hanging coats: add one to each block. Make sure there's enough room to move around them. It'd be awfully disappointing to find a doorway to another world, only to be thwarted by a denim jacket.

4 ONLY ONE more bit to do, and then you can go frolic in the Narnian snow to your heart's content. Promise. Blend the very end of the corridor into the woods by replacing some of the wooden floor with podzol, scattering ferns and grass throughout, and adding some snow patches for good measure. Vines creeping up the walls can also be effective in blending it in. Your wardrobe is now complete (and it's only slightly more complicated than an IKEA flatpack). But at least you've got no bits left over.

5 **SO YOU'RE** finally in the fantasy forest of Narnia, but without a landmark, it could be tricky to find your way home. The solution: recreate the famous lamp-post. First, stack a few fence posts on top of each other, and balance a glowstone on top of them. Next, attach a trapdoor to each side of the glowstone, then close all of them (it's oddly satisfying). To finish it off, put a wooden slab on top, and four fence posts around the bottom of the glowstone. Sorted!

6 **IN THE** Lion, The Witch And The Wardrobe, Father Christmas kits out Peter, Susan and Lucy with some awesome weaponry. He arrives in a sleigh, which you can build with more of those handy-dandy fence posts and some red wool. The sleigh should be slightly deeper at the back end, as that's where the jolly dude stashes his deadly presents. Peter gets a sword, Susan a bow, and Lucy a healing potion (none for you, Edmund, you traitor). Throw 'em in the sleigh, ready for action.

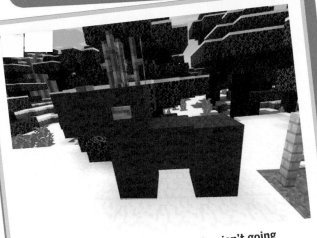

7 **BUT HANG** about! That thing isn't going anywhere without a few reindeer to pull it. Got wool? Buttons? Iron bars? Then you've got yourself a reindeer. Construct an upside-down U-shape out of five blocks of brown wool, and add on a two-block head. A button on each side makes its eyes, and one on top makes a nose. The antlers are iron bars. Use carpet in any colour to add a fancy saddle, and hook them up to the sleigh with even more fence posts.

8 **WARDROBE: CHECK.** Witch: not so much. Lion: definitely not. One out of three isn't bad, but you can do better than that. While Minecraft witches are less glamorous than Narnia's White Witch, they do have rad wiggly noses. The corresponding spawn egg will provide you with your witch. Now, what about that lion? Well, it's no Aslan, but an ocelot is the closest thing you have to the king of the jungle. Crack open another spawn egg, and let the battle commence!

DIARY OF SURVIVAL ISLAND

Cranking it up a Notch with one of Minecraft's toughest challenges

▶ THE CHALLENGE...

EVER WISHED you could just get away from it all and make a fresh start on a desert island? Well here's a challenge for you: set Minecraft to Hardcore difficulty, start on an island seed with nothing but a few trees, grass and sugar cane, and eventually battle the Ender Dragon... without a single death.

Victory will mean mad XP and a dragon egg fry-up for everyone; failure, the immediate deletion of the world save. We've done it, and kept a Survival Diary of what happened to help you along. Will the race to The End, er, drag on? Or will it be cruelly cut short by a stray zombie? Read on, find out, and be inspired to explore your own survival island. 1

▶ DAY ONE   MOOD: OPTIMISTIC

WAIT, WHERE am I? Oh, not again! Well, at least they left me with my shoes this time. Best get cracking.

I spring into action like a cubic ninja, punching trees into splintery submission. Grass is next: yield your riches, pixelated pasture! One set of seeds?! My stomach is eating itself already.

Scanning the island 2 (a process that takes half a second) reveals a handful of friendly and potentially delicious animals to get acquainted with. I make direct, purposeful eye contact with a pig as I craft a wooden sword. Dominance asserted.

The setting sun saves his bacon, because I must dig a dirt bunker to hide in, lest any mobs decide to spawn all over my survivalist hopes and dreams. A sunrise and a few blocks of cobblestone later, 3 I've built a furnace. The pig is trying very hard to hide, but a rabbit practically leaps into my waiting oven. What a team player. You seeing this, pig? You're first on my list, buddy. Just you wait...

DAY TWO MOOD: REALISTIC

SAPLINGS ARE planted and seeds are sown, but now I'm grubby, tired, and starving – and it's raining. Perfect. Gritting my teeth, I begin the lengthy process of hollowing out my crude hole in the ground to turn it into a mine. 4 The smell of smoke fills the air, and the thought of BBQ teases my mind, as the furnace burns wood into charcoal for my torches. The pig lasts five minutes before I pork chop him into bite-size pieces. RIP, Peppa. You can't say you weren't expecting it.

A full stack of cobblestone gathered, I begin the construction of my epic fortress. There's sand as far as the eye can see, so windows aren't an issue. 5 After a brief flirtation with the idea of a skylight (I abandon this, deciding that summoning Kevin McCloud would only mean another mouth to feed), I plump for a spiral staircase. A full moon rises as I stack up steps and lay out the second floor of my base. I long for bed. 6

THE RULES...

1. Play on at least Normal difficulty. Hardcore difficulty is a great test for Minecraft veterans: you get one life, there are no respawns, and your world save disappears if you die. Starving to death is possible, but backing out isn't, as you can't change the difficulty setting.

2. Start on an island seed (duh!). There are some great ones to be found on the Internet. For an authentic challenge, use an island that has only a few trees and some grass.

3. No island-hopping! You've got to survive on your island with what little you have, and players who gather resources from elsewhere will be fed to the Wither. You've been warned.

DAY THREE MOOD: LONELY

AS IF being hungry and sleep-deprived wasn't enough, I'm desperately lonely. My companion count has recently decreased by one – burp – and even the rabbits are keeping their distance now. Fine, be that way! I'm off to the mine, losers. Almost instantly, I dig up some iron, and can't wait to go rub it in their furry faces – but I also dig up a creeper 7. No armour, no respawns: no chance. I get outta there, hopping all the way back up the stairs to the surface.

This is when I suspect that I'm starting to go a bit wrong in the head: I see a cow. And then another cow. And two sheep. What is going on? The entire cast of Babe has turned up in my absence 8. Am I hallucinating? No, it would appear not. The torches on my island must have helped spawn them. I totally meant to do that. Totally.

I can now make a farm and breed animals for food. Every animal is precious, so obviously I immediately kill a sheep, and dye its wool to make myself a fluffy friend. Think I'll call him Wilson. 9

▶️ DAY FOUR   MOOD: HUNGRY

HERDING THE cows and sheep into a pen isn't easy without a sheaf of tempting wheat, but I manage it with a few encouraging shoves 🔟. Once the harvest comes in, breeding them will be a doddle, but I can't afford to kill any right now. I've got one pork chop left, and a couple of apples to wash it down with. My hunger bar is satisfied: my soul is not.

I set to work crafting iron armour from my bountiful ore: in hardcore survival modes, the best offence is a good defence. Offence is a pretty good offence as well, though, so I waste no time in whipping up a lovely, sharp iron sword 🔟1. But that mine won't excavate itself. I fling myself back down into it, and run headlong into a skeleton 🔟2. Okay, let's run through my options. Number one: run. Number two: wee myself. Number three: give him a good walloping. With my trusty iron gear, I avoid a combination of one and two, winning the battle – and some bones into the bargain.

▶️ DAY FIVE   MOOD: £££

ENCOURAGED BY my skellybob success, I decide to stay another day in the mine, plowing through the cobblestone like a Hungry Hippo. All at once, I run smack into a cluster of diamonds 🔟3.

DIAMONDS! Before I've even managed to make bread! Priorities, am I right? I've never been punched in the mouth by a precious gem before, but it feels pretty darn sweet. Time to take 'em home to my woolly orange pal. 🔟4

Wilson doesn't really react when I show off my haul, and I'm a bit annoyed, until I remember he doesn't actually have a face. Shrugging and turning away, I do some mental maths and figure out that ten diamonds is enough for a pickaxe and a sword, with plenty left over for an enchanting table. Result.

The sun starts to rise over my bone-mealed farm 🔟5, and I can almost taste the freshly-baked bread as I survey my empire. "Everything the light touches is ours, Wilson", I tell him. He didn't reply. Again.

▌ DAY SIX   MOOD: COCKY

THIS SURVIVAL island lark is well easy, innit? Wheat and sugar farm on the go, torches keeping nasty mobs away and speeding up crop growth, enough bling to cement my status as Island Swagmaster **16** (there are no prizes for second place, Wilson)... Piece of cake. Well, I haven't quite managed cake yet, but steak I can definitely grab me a piece of.

I saunter over to my cow and sheep pen and start making it rain wheat. Breeding my two sheep will produce enough wool for me to make a bed – I haven't slept in days, but at least it's not affecting my mind... hatstands! Doughnuts. Creme brulee? Quite. Once my cows have produced offspring **17**, I make one of them into mincemeat. A hiss interrupts my evening meal. I turn around, to be greeted by... Well, just look at the picture. A spider is all up in my grill **18** (and my grilled meat). Fortunately, I survive, thanks to a mixture of smacking it over the head with a steak, and hysterical crying. It's a dark reminder of the danger that lurks all around.

▌ DAY SEVEN   MOOD: DOMESTIC

AH, THE seventh day. The traditional day of rest. I decide to spend the day pottering about the island and generally avoiding any bother. A few more trees have sprung up, meaning I can make signs and name some of the island landmarks. The farm is christened Slaughterhouse V-eal **19** (Wilson's a Vonnegut fan), and the fortress Casa del GamesMaster **20**, because everything sounds more impressive in Spanish.

I lay out a gravel path between the fortress, the farm, the mine, and my crops. It crunches underfoot as I carefully pluck the island's flowers, replanting them in neat rows in front of my home sweet home. For my interior, sticks and wool create a tasteful skull painting **21**, which also serves as a handy reminder of my imminent death. Yay!

My day of rest is rounded out in the best possible way: I can finally make a bed. Crawling under the covers, I consider giving up the Ender Dragon pipe dream. This is heaven.

▌ DAY EIGHT   MOOD: TORMENTED

I HATE Mondays, I think, as a worrying number of eyes cast a red glow from a shadowy void in my mine **22**. My sword makes swift work of the spider – but like his brother before him, he doesn't even have the decency to drop string. No bow and arrow for me, then. But that's the least of my worries: I fight off two zombies and a creeper from the same horrible hole before I retreat to the surface, heart pounding and health low.

I'm not even safe in my own home. A skeleton sloshes through the water behind my fortress, and I have trouble getting up close as it peppers me with arrows. It's soon impaled on the business end of my sword, but it's managed to fire an arrow into the business end of me **23**. Ouch.

As luck would have it I've finally got leftover wheat to make bread, and it's been a bad day at the office, so I do what I always do when I'm sad: go home and eat quite a lot of cheese. **24**

▶ DAY NINE   MOOD: ADVENTUROUS

MOBS DON'T scare me! I refuse to cower in my fortress like a big, blocky baby. Instead, I'll speed around on the high seas in my trusty boat **25**. Yes, I know I'm not allowed to set foot on any other land. I'm just looking.

My desire for a wander satisfied and feet back on solid ground, I have a thought. My torches are keeping mobs at bay – but I'll need endermen to spawn. They drop ender pearls, which are key to getting to The End. The solution: create an unlit platform that will trap enemies. I surround Mobs 'R' Us with fences **26**, dreaming foolish dreams of browsing its dangerous wares like my own personal supermarket, cool music playing in the background. Nice.

For now, I start hunting my lanky prey underground. I very quickly spot purple sparkles, and when more endermen join the party, I'm left clutching more pearls than an affronted 1940s housewife. Brainwave number two arrives: to craft the Eyes of Ender that point me to The End, I must make blaze powder. Which comes from blaze rods. Which come from the Nether. Gulp. **27**

▶ DAY TEN   MOOD: BETRAYED

I MIGHT as well start mining the obsidian to make a Nether portal while I'm down here. Diamond pickaxe: check. Buckets of water: check. Now for some lava **28**. There's a sticky bubbling somewhere nearby – I grind through cobblestone and catch sight of a few orange drops plopping thickly through the block ahead. I hold my breath, carefully revealing a large pool of lava that could easily turn me into a chargrilled chump. Dumping water on it creates obsidian, and I mine ten blocks to make my personal portal to hell.

I fancy that's enough peril for one day, so it's back up to the island for animal-breeding and a lovely meal of mutton. But it's anarchy at Slaughterhouse V-eal: the cows rush at me when I open the gate **29**. I dole out justice via my new diamond sword, gaining some leather in the process. Furious, I storm off and begin making books **30**; an enchanting table will be helpful once I'm up against the dragon. May this beautifully-bound book serve as a lesson to you all, traitorous cows.

▶ DAY ELEVEN   MOOD: RELUCTANT

YEAH, I could build the Nether today, but I've got no bow and, er... Mobs 'R' Us needs upgrading! It's not attracted a single enderman **31** so that most likely means it should be bigger and darker. Perhaps higher walls will block out more light and increase spawns: there are still more ender pearls to collect if I want a shot at finding that stronghold.

Time to build the portal? Well, um... you've got to stop and smell the roses at some point, right? I think I'll just dawdle about the island. Admire the scenery. My mine needs a name **32**. Very important work – crucial, actually. Right, that's done.

Let me stop you there, before you ask about building that thing again, because Wilson has been woefully neglected as of late **33**. We take a lovely stroll along the beach (well, he just sort of sits there and I walk around him). Alright, I'm losing the plot! Can you blame me?

DAY TWELVE MOOD: BRAVE

I KNOW, I know. I've got to do it. Putting together a Nether portal is dismally simple: a vague rectangle of obsidian and death. With my flint and steel, I light that sucker up, and all manner of unsettling noises emanate from the infernal dimension beyond **34**. A shudder runs through me.

There's no reason to panic. Sure, I've only got one life, and there's a chance I could spawn right into lava... I shake that thought off, thinking of those much-needed blaze rods, and decide to get practical. Iron armour on, diamond gear ready, plenty of food, buckets of water, torches: I kit out my hotbar with all the essentials **35**. Obviously, Wilson gets a spot – if we go down, we go down together.

Hopefully it'll be a largely uneventful trip. I step into the portal. I've got a solid set of armour, a diamond sword, and the most powerful weapon of all: friendship. What could go wrong?

EXTRA CHALLENGE?

1. The Veggie – Don't eat any meat!
2. Big Softie – Only use wooden tools and leather armour.
3. Sleep Is For The Weak – No beds allowed!
4. Pacifist – Don't kill any mobs except endermen and the Ender Dragon.
5. Itty-Bitty Island – Survive on a 10x10 island.

35

37

36

34

DAY THIRTEEN MOOD: UNLUCKY

UPDATE: EVERYTHING GOING WRONG, EVERYTHING ON FIRE. Whilst I haven't spawned into lava, it's all over the place **36**: flowing in waterfalls from the ceiling; gurgling ominously below my narrow pathways in vast lakes; setting fire to the Netherrack underneath my feet. Each step could be my last. I grip Wilson tightly. In my head he lets out a reassuring sigh. Only in my head, mind.

Focusing on my goal of finding a Nether fortress, and therefore blazes, I sneak past many a zombie pigman. The search is fruitless. I lose track of time, and, convinced I hear the creepy wheezing of blazes, dash off into the distance. Nothing – and now I'm totally lost.

Just when I conclude that it might be a good time to build a base somewhere, a massive black blob comes hurtling at me at speed. A giant magma cube?! Really, Nether? Wait... Does this mean that there might be a fortress around here?

DAY ??? MOOD: HELP ME!

WHAT HAPPENED? What day is it? Ugh, I must have been knocked out by that magma cube. The fortress! I was close! I spin around, but everything feels unfamiliar. For instance, there certainly wasn't a gang of zombie pigmen surrounding me before. As I search for a way out of the ambush zone, a friendly-looking light flickers in the distance. I squint at it.

Next thing I know, it smacks me square in my flammable face. UNFRIENDLY LIGHT. GHAST FIREBALL. It's too dark to make out the weird floating mob, but I can hear its harrowing demon-baby cooing as it rapid-fires at me. I've got no bow to shoot it with, and my health is dipping fast, so I swing my sword wildly in an effort to deflect its projectiles back at it. The zombie pigmen find this to be highly impolite, and decide that my immediate evisceration is fair punishment. The ghast finishes me off with a fireball. I'm dead. Cooked like a well done steak **37**. My old cows would be having a good laugh at me.

37

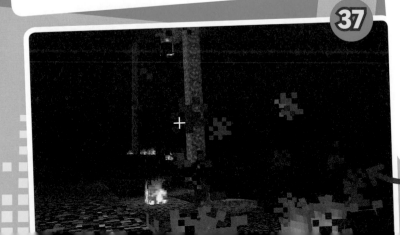

PUZZLES

Test your brain with these teasers...

ANSWERS ON PAGE 93

GUESS THE MOBS!

CAN YOU tell these mobs from their shadows? Write the name of each in the space provided, then flip over to page 92 to check if you were right!

1

I'm a...

....

2

I'm a...

....

3

I'm a...

....

4

I'm a...

....

5

I'm a...

....

6

I'm a...

....

KNOW YOUR BIOMES
SUNFLOWER PLAINS

IF EVER THERE was a biome generated specifically for two sweethearts to bound across before a springtime embrace, then it's this one. Flat, and peppered with those sunny yellow flowers, these plains are the only place you'll find naturally spawning sunflowers. Alongside dandelions, these can be used to obtain yellow dye.

HAVING TROUBLE FINDING A USE FOR THE HUMBLE SUNFLOWER? WELL KNOWING THAT THESE YELLOW CHAPS WILL ALWAYS FACE EAST IS USEFUL FOR NAVIGATION.

DON'T BOTHER TRYING TO PLACE A SUNFLOWER IN A PLANT POT. THEY'RE TWO BLOCKS TALL AND SO, MUCH LIKE PEONIES AND LILACS, WON'T FIT.

WHILE OTHER FLOWERS TEND TO COME ACROSS AS PIXELATED MESSES OF COLOUR, SUNFLOWERS ARE EASY TO RECOGNISE, DUE TO THEIR PERFECTLY ROUND SHAPE.

MEGA MINECRAFT QUIZ!

How much do you really know about your favourite game?

INFO

MEGA MINECRAFT QUIZ

TIME NEEDED: 30 MINUTES
EXTRA INFO: SET A TIMER –
CAN YOU ANSWER ALL THE
QUESTIONS IN TIME?

LET'S BE honest: even your nanna could probably identify a creeper by now. "Is it that scuttly green thing, dear? Ooh, I don't care for him. Best make sure he doesn't go boom." Of course, if you consider yourself to be a Minecraft fan, your knowledge should probably go a few blocks deeper than that. So take our quiz, and test your trivia smarts…

1 What is the name of this block?
- ☐ **A.** Redstone
- ☐ **B.** Glowstone
- ☐ **C.** Cobblestone

2 What light levels do you need to maintain in order to prevent creepers from spawning?
- ☐ **A.** 8
- ☐ **B.** 4
- ☐ **C.** 11

3 Which of these materials is the hardest?
- ☐ **A.** Iron
- ☐ **B.** Gold
- ☐ **C.** Obsidian

4 How many adjacent blocks can be powered by one block of redstone?
- [ ] **A.** 4
- [ ] **B.** 2
- [ ] **C.** 1

5 How many biomes are there in total?
- [ ] **A.** 22
- [ ] **B.** 10
- [ ] **C.** 75

6 What do you get if you cross a cow and a toadstool?
- [ ] **A.** Mooshroom
- [ ] **B.** Killer bunny
- [ ] **C.** Nightmares

I LOVE WATCHING MOOOOVIES!

7 In what year was the first alpha version of Minecraft released?
- [ ] **A.** 2001
- [ ] **B.** 2009
- [ ] **C.** 2011

8 How many platforms has Minecraft been released on in total?
- [ ] **A.** 17
- [ ] **B.** 8
- [ ] **C.** 12

9 What is the name of the female player character?
- [ ] **A.** Joanne
- [ ] **B.** Stevena
- [ ] **C.** Alex

WHY OH WHY DIDN'T THEY GIVE ME SHOES?

10 What is the missing ingredient in this cake recipe: sugar, egg, wheat...?
- [ ] **A.** Flour
- [ ] **B.** Water
- [ ] **C.** Milk

11 What is Minecraft creator Notch's real name?
- [ ] **A.** Markus
- [ ] **B.** Jens Bergensten
- [ ] **C.** Daniel Frisk

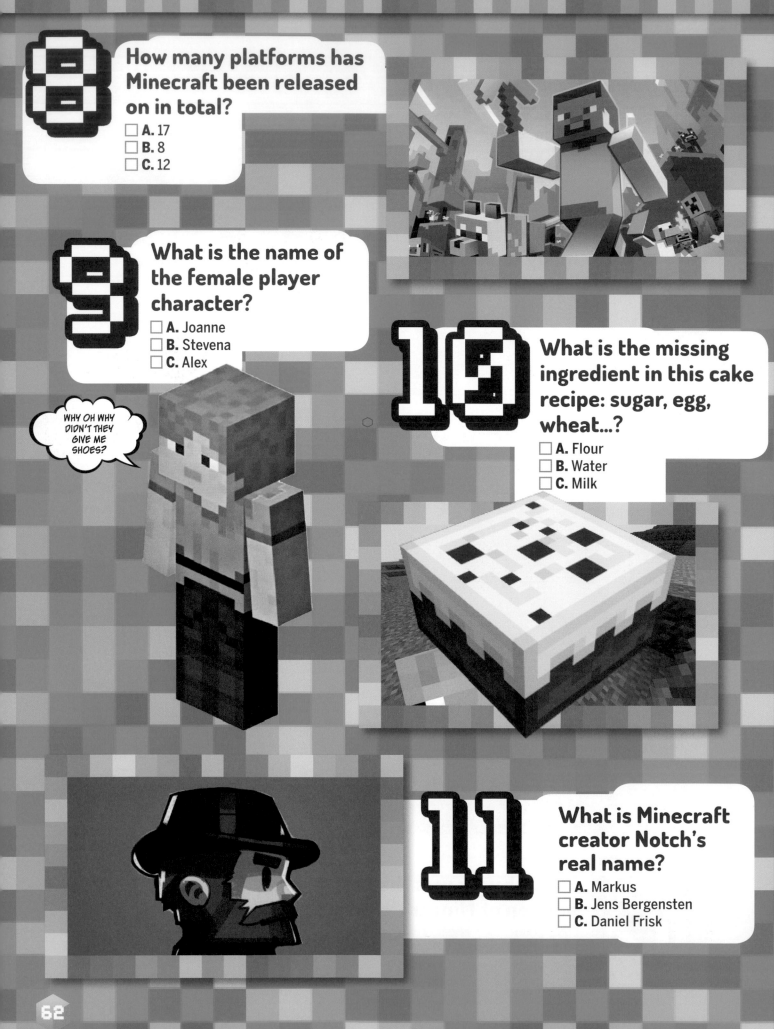

12

What is the name of the infamous 'ghost' (who does not exist) that some people have claimed to see in Minecraft?

- ☐ **A.** Zerowine
- ☐ **B.** Herobrine
- ☐ **C.** Spectral Gary

13

Which British politician was turned into a Minecraft character?

- ☐ **A.** David Cameron
- ☐ **B.** Ed Miliband
- ☐ **C.** Boris Johnson

IT'S NOT SLIME... IT'S BOGEYS!

14

Where would you find a zombie pigman?

- ☐ **A.** Forest biome
- ☐ **B.** The Nether
- ☐ **C.** The End

15

What colour eyes do villagers have?
- ☐ **A.** Green
- ☐ **B.** Blue
- ☐ **C.** Brown

16

How many items can you fit in a single chest?
- ☐ **A.** 25
- ☐ **B.** 27
- ☐ **C.** 32

I WISH I COULD FLY... RIGHT UP TO THE SKY!

17

What kind of mobs are squid?
- ☐ **A.** Hostile
- ☐ **B.** Passive
- ☐ **C.** Neutral

BUT I'M ACTUALLY A REALLY NICE GUY!

18 Which of these will not stop an enderman from attacking you?

- ☐ **A.** Not looking at them
- ☐ **B.** Wearing a jack o'lantern
- ☐ **C.** Standing still while staring at them

19 Which of these is the most sensible weapon against the Ender Dragon?

- ☐ **A.** Bow and arrows
- ☐ **B.** Sword
- ☐ **C.** Axe

20 What was Minecraft's original title?

- ☐ **A.** Block Digger
- ☐ **B.** Cave Game
- ☐ **C.** Special Steve's Subterranean Adventure

HOW HAVE YOU DONE? CHECK THE ANSWERS...

ANSWERS

10: C	20: B
9: C	19: A
8: A	18: C
7: B	17: B
6: A	16: B
5: C	15: A
4: A	14: B
3: C	13: C
2: A	12: B
1: B	11: A

WHAT KIND OF MINECRAFTER ARE YOU?

0-5: Skeleton
Not many Minecraft facts in your mind, are there? Must try harder!

6-10: Villager
You know the lay of the land, but you're not the most adventurous.

11-15: Creeper
You may not be the main man, but you still pack an explosive punch.

16-20: Steve
Top of the blocks. You know the game inside out – well done!

THE CAT'S WHISKERS

Get to know the YouTube superstar better with our smashing Stampy special

YES, EVEN CATS CAN WEAR DIAMOND ARMOUR!

C hances are, if you're reading this gloriously chunky Minecraft annual, you know who Stampy is. You've watched his videos, shared his adventures, perhaps even bought his lovely book. But for anyone who doesn't play Minecraft, he's a bit of a mystery. Many folk could easily stroll past Stampy in the street, unaware they almost rubbed shoulders with a YouTube superstar; a man who gets more YouTube hits than many successful pop stars, with a legion of dedicated, block-bashing followers. Many mainstream newspapers and websites run bemused stories, struggling to understand why we tune in to watch hours of pretend things being built in a virtual world. Of course, anyone who's watched Stampy's videos – or played Minecraft themselves – will know why.

That's why the next few pages are dedicated to Stampy, whose real name is Joseph Garrett. We were lucky enough to interview him, and naturally we asked him for all his closely guarded YouTube secrets. While they might not be enough to propel us to internet superstardom, his top ten tips are still a smashing place to start. Whether it's YouTube tips, Stampy's favourite Minecraft block or his proudest achievements, we've got it covered. On top of that, we've also got a list of essential Stampy facts that everyone should know – some familiar, others less so. If you're already a fan, slice yourself a whopping great piece of cake, sit back and enjoy; if not, hopefully we can convince you to give Stampy's lovely channel a look.

STAMPY FACTS

He's one of YouTube's biggest stars, but how much do we really know about Stampy? Well, rather a lot, actually. Here is a list of some fascinating Stampy tidbits, including his rise to stardom, spin-off channels and motivation. For ease, we refer to Stampy and Joseph as the same person – it can get confusing with two names!

01 Stampy's channel was one of the fastest growing channels of any genre on YouTube. He currently averages around 3,500 new subscribers every single day – more than enough to fill Wembley Stadium every month!

02 His daily views are pretty crazy and impressive, too. His videos average over four million daily views – that's way more than the entire population of Berlin, or all of Georgia, in a single day!

IS THIS A GIGANTIC STAMPY STATUE, OR JUST PERSPECTIVE?

STAMPY SPEAKS OUT

Inspiration, advice and tasty Minecraft tips from the YouTube superstar

You don't become a YouTube success overnight. As well as years of hard work, epic levels of dedication and a charming demeanour, you also need to be really rather good at your game of choice. With this in mind, we recently got the chance to chat to Stampy about his greatest successes, inspiration and the secret to succeeding at YouTube.

We also discuss more technical stuff, such as why Minecraft is such a great fit for YouTube videos. We're a bit greedy, so we also asked him for his top ten tips for Minecraft success. And because he's a thoroughly decent sort, he was kind enough to oblige us. Stampy's tips are ideal for refining your game or preparing you for a lucrative career as a Minecrafting YouTube superstar. Heed his advice, and remember your ol' friends on the Minecraft Annual 2020 team if you ever become YouTube billionaires...

03 Stampy uploads new videos every day – he just can't get enough of video making! This can often take many hours to make and upload. It might look like the best job in the world, but it's still really hard work.

04 In December 2013, Stampy's channel was temporarily terminated by Google. After petitions, outrage, and the #SaveStampy hashtag trending on Twitter, Google apologised and reinstated his channel. To this day, we don't know why it was terminated. Perhaps they don't like men who think they're cats?

05 Stampy didn't start off making Minecraft videos. Instead, he recorded amusing real-life movies, as well as stop-motion animation. The name Stampylonghead comes from one of these animations.

06 Joseph studied video production at college and university. As uni work began to take up loads of his time, he set up the Stampylonghead channel to upload less time-consuming Let's Play videos. The rest is YouTube history.

07 His first gaming videos weren't all about Minecraft, either. He started off recording commentaries over games such as Call of Duty and Halo. His first go at Minecraft was on the Xbox 360 version.

Can you remember your first experience of Minecraft? What was it that got you hooked?
My first experience with Minecraft was my first episode in My Lovely World. It is a long running series that I still do to this day. The complete freedom and possibilities were what got me hooked.

What is it about Minecraft – and specifically, your Minecraft videos – that inspires and engages so many people?
I think that people mainly enjoy the humour and stories that I tell in my videos. They also come as a source of inspiration when they might not be sure what they want to build.

Minecraft has an active and engaged community, perhaps more so than any other game. Why do you think this is?
I think the Minecraft audience has stayed engaged for so long because there is always something new to do in the game. The community and developers are always adding something new.

Why is YouTube so important for Minecraft?
YouTube is so important to Minecraft because for many it is where they first hear about Minecraft. It is the most popular videogame on YouTube and helps to spread the word about the game. I think it also encourages people to continue to play because they want to replicate what they see in videos.

"I THINK PEOPLE MAINLY ENJOY THE HUMOUR AND STORIES I TELL IN MY VIDEOS"

08 Before becoming a YouTube hit, Joseph was a barman. He left his job to focus solely on videos when he started earning enough to do it for a living. At the time, he was on 10,000 subscribers, rather than the nine million he's got now.

09 He's doing amazingly well now, but his beginnings were reassuringly humble: Joseph started out filming in his bedroom at his parents' house.

10 Joseph met his buddy iBallisticSquid in January 2013. They became fast friends and YouTube collaborators, and have a joint channel called The Magic Animal Club.

11 In a display of parental awesomeness, Joseph's parents were happy for him to live rent-free until he could develop his channel into a full time career. Thanks, Mr & Mrs Garrett!

"IT'S A LOT MORE FUN TO PUT ALL YOUR ENERGY INTO MAKING GREAT VIDEOS"

What's the most difficult thing you've ever built?
The most difficult thing I have built is a working treadmill. I also spent a lot of time building a giant frog that I am rather proud of.

What's your proudest Minecraft achievement?
My proudest Minecraft achievement is My Lovely World. I have been building it for so long, and I am proud that I am able to continue coming up with ideas for new things to add.

If you could give your fans one piece of advice about becoming a YouTuber, what would it be?
My advice for being a YouTuber is to focus on the videos and not YouTube. It is easy to get overwhelmed with YouTube stats and trying to get views. It's a lot more fun to put all of your energy just into making great videos.

You're obviously a huge gamer, and your videos aren't just about Minecraft. Has the games industry changed since you started doing this?
The gaming industry has changed in so many ways since I have started. YouTube (and YouTubers) have really started having an impact on the success of games. You can see many more games targeted directly at

YouTubers in the hope that they will play the game. The rise of free to play and mobile games is also having dramatic effects on the entire industry.

How did you come up with the name 'Stampy Longhead'?
It was originally the name of a character in an animation I made at school.

How long does it take you to make each of your videos in total?
Some series I can record several videos in one day. Bigger videos can take over a week of work on just one video. 95% of what I do is planning.

What is your favourite Minecraft block and why?
My favourite block to build out of is sandstone because not many people use it and I love the texture and colour. It also reminds me of white chocolate.

What's been your favourite quest in Minecraft?
My favourite quest in My Lovely World was probably in the episode "Cat to the Future". I make the world's tastiest cake and go back in time so I can eat it more than once. I accidently go back too far and end up in an epic adventure. ∎

12 Want more awesome facts? The logo on Joseph's channel, featuring Mr Stampy Cat, was designed by his father, and his mum helps run his Facebook page.

13 Stampy's audience is largely comprised of six to 14-year-olds, and the majority of them are girls. Even then, it's a pretty even 60/40 split, proving, if it were even necessary, that Minecraft is for everyone.

14 Stampy gets well over 3000 messages a day – far more than he can physically answer. They're not just about Minecraft, either. Sometimes, his fans just tell him how their day went!

15 Want to understand how big Stampy is? Well, in 2014, he had the fourth biggest channel on YouTube – wedged between pop gigastars Katy Perry and Shakira. Lovely!

THE QUEST FOR TASTY CAKE TAKES STAMPY TO SPOOKY PLACES

16 Because Stampy's videos are aimed at a specific audience, he makes sure it's all family friendly. You won't find any bad language, and the emphasis is on good, clean, creative fun.

17 Stampy now has a second channel, called Wonder Quest. It features a 12-episode show of the same name. It's still made in Minecraft, but the production values are snazzier, and it's more educational. Wonderful!

18 Wonder Quest draws on Joseph's previous experience in video production. It's completely scripted – rather than the spontaneous stuff in his other shows – and even features original music and sound effects.

19 Every episode of Wonder Quest has an educational angle. In order to overcome a particular challenge, Stampy usually has to learn something new. Suddenly, the name makes a lot of sense!

20 The spin-off channel also features the I Wonder cartoon series – more traditional animation that digs deeper into the educational themes of Wonder Quest. Thankfully, entertainment is still the most important aspect.

TOP 10 TIPS FROM STAMPY

Polish your Minecraft skills with Stampy's handy tips

1 Sleep tight. On your first night make sure your number one priority is to make a bed. You don't want to be caught outside in the dark when the googlies spawn. Make a bed and sleep as soon as it starts to get dark.

2 Make sure you always use the right tool for the job. Start by making a wooden pickaxe so you can gather cobblestone, then make a set of stone tools. Once you have iron you can upgrade. Make sure you use an iron pickaxe to mine diamonds. Using the wrong tool to destroy a block is slow and will eventually destroy the tool.

3 Don't get lost. Create a map and make a note of where your house is. When exploring a cave leave a trail of torches behind you so you can follow them to get back out. Do the same when exploring the Nether. You can also look at the sun or moon to work out which way is North. When in a cave you can examine the texture of cobblestone to find out which way is North.

4 Don't go hungry. One of the first things you should do in a new world is get a good supply of food. The easiest way to get food at first is to find meat. Once you have a house, making a wheat farm should be a top priority. Eventually you can also plant carrots and potatoes. If you want something tastier then make a cake!

5 Protect your house from googlies. Keeping the area around your house bright is very important. The googlies only spawn when it's dark. You could also dig a pit around your base that the googlies can't jump over. Setting up traps can also be helpful, just be careful not to get caught in them yourself!

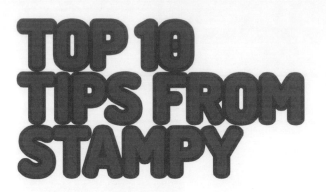

21 Stampy's collaborators in Wonder Quest include CaptainSparklez, AmyLee33, EvanTubeHD, ShayCarl, and his real-life buddy iBallisticSquid – all Minecraft superstars in their own right.

22 Wonder Quest has been a huge success. The channel has more than 135 million views, with two seasons to enjoy. I Wonder has even been used as an educational tool in some schools.

23 Stampy isn't just huge on YouTube, either – he has over 600,000 followers on Twitter and more than 700,000 Likes on Facebook. Give us a retweet, Stampy!

24 Stampy's first video was published in May 2012, but the tone is slightly different from the ones we know and love today – instead, his early videos are more like direct, traditional game reviews.

25 Stampy deliberately keeps his personal life separate from his YouTube videos. This is partly because Minecraft is more fun, but also because he considers himself a video producer, not a vlogger.

6 Get diamonds. Diamonds are probably the most precious and useful item in the game. To find them you need to dig right down to the bottom of the world. It is much easier to find them when in a natural cave but is safer to find them when digging in a straight line. When you find diamonds it's best to go home or put them in a chest to make sure they stay safe.

7 Learn redstone. Lots of people are scared to try and learn how redstone works but it can be really useful. Try experimenting with it to see what it can do. Try making a doorbell or use pistons to make a secret doorway. It can also make very useful things that make your life much easier.

8 Get creative. You can get bored of playing Minecraft if you don't have an idea for something to build. If you don't know what to build try building your house or school. Building giant versions of your favourite characters is fun too. If you still don't know what to build try watching one of my videos and try re-building what I build, but do it in your own style.

9 Play with friends. Minecraft can get lonely when playing by yourself. Inviting friends can make it lots more fun. Work on a project together or compete against each other in challenges. If you are on a PC you can go on a server and play with 1000s of people. Just be careful to only talk to people that you know in real life.

10 Defeat the dragon. Defeating the Ender Dragon is one of the toughest challenges in Minecraft. Before entering The End make sure you are 100% prepared for the battle. Bring lots of food and equipment. You want at least a full set of iron armour but diamond would be better. You want a bow and LOTS of arrows. Putting a pumpkin on your head means that the Endermen won't attack you unless you attack them first. You also want to bring blocks that can be used to pile up. Once you enter The End you can't leave until you have defeated the dragon. Good luck!

Stampy's Lovely Book is Joseph Garrett's first official book, and it's available from Egmont Publishing for £7.99

26 Joseph has also appeared on mainstream TV. As well as doing interviews, he was a judge on the CBBC series Appsolute Genius – part of the BBC's Make it Digital initiative, aimed at inspiring a new generation of coders.

27 Joseph's videos are made using the console version of Minecraft, but he'd like to see more parity between platforms – things like cross-platform play and shareable levels.

28 Despite being a superstar, Joseph isn't a massive fan of crowds: thankfully, he's okay being on stage in front of his legions of viewers, though (not to mention the millions watching at home).

29 Stampy was friends with most of his YouTube collaborators before he became famous – they're people who knew each other in real life, and got into YouTube together, which is exactly why his collaborations work so well.

30 Despite being based in a sleepy part of England, Stampy is an international success: 50% of his viewers are based in the US, and 25% are from the UK.

KNOW YOUR BIOMES
VILLAGES

WITH RANDOMLY CREATED, fully-formed structures, villages are often the most exciting of the biomes to stumble into. They're inhabited by large-nosed villagers who happily go about their own business during the day. You can even trade with them in the PC version. However, zombies will frequently invade during the night and knock down doors to infect the natives, so you'll have to fight to protect them or destroy the zombie spawn point. Not quite Resident Evil 4's village scene, but close enough...

NEED TORCHES EARLY IN THE GAME? TAKING A COUPLE FROM THE BUILDINGS CAN HELP UNTIL YOU HAVE THE MATERIALS TO MAKE YOUR OWN.

CHECK THE BLACKSMITH'S HOUSE AND YOU'LL OFTEN FIND A CHEST FILLED WITH GOODIES (USUALLY RARE METALS) FOR YOU TO STEAL.

VILLAGES USUALLY HAVE READY-MADE WHEAT FARMS RIPE FOR HARVESTING. YOU'LL BE ABLE TO MAKE BREAD IN NO TIME.

GAMES MASTER PRESENTS

MINECRAFT TIPS CARDS!

CUT OUT AND KEEP EXPERT TIPS CARDS

HOW DOES STEVE KEEP FIT?

HE RUNS AROUND THE BLOCK!

BLOCK Diamond

YOU can find the rare diamond mineral by mining Diamond Ore, or from scavaging Loot Chests. The best armour and weapons in the game are made from Diamond, so you'll be a Minecraft legend if you find some!

ITEM Sugar

MADE from Sugar Cane, Sugar is used in Minecraft for brewing and cooking. Bizarrely, kill a Witch and she will drop anything up to six blocks of Sugar! Wow, I didn't know Witches had a sweet tooth!

MOB Wolf

YOU don't get regular fluffy dogs in Minecraft, instead you can tame the local wolves and make them your pets. Be careful when they are in the wild though – they're not friendly, and if you attack them they will bite back!

WEAPON Shield

COMING in 16 colours at the last count, Shields are the perfect way to protect yourself in a battle. You can make a Shield by crafting any type of wood you can get your hands on, and an Iron Ingot.

FOOD Sweet Berries

WHERE can you find Sweet Berries? Why, in Sweet Berry Bushes of course! The longer the bush has had to grow, the more berries you will get from it. If you are off on a berry hunt, try the Taiga biome.

VEHICLE Minecart with TNT

WHAT? Why would you want to put a block of TNT inside a Minecart?! Well they can be useful for setting off timed explosions with activator rails further along a track. They will not damage the rails, just everything else!

GAMES MASTER PRESENTS

MINECRAFT TIPS CARDS!

▌▶ BECOME A MINECRAFT EXPERT!

GET YOUR safety scissors at the ready because we've created eight pages of Minecraft tips cards especially for you. 33 cards in total, written by Minecraft experts. Covering Blocks, Items, Mobs, Weapons, Food, Vehicles and more! All you need to do is cut them out by carefully cutting along the dotted lines (round off the corners if you like). Then keep them handy the next time you play!

WHY NOT CUT OUT THE CARDS AND PLAY A TOP TRUMPS-STYLE GAME?!

GAMES MASTER PRESENTS
MINECRAFT TIPS CARDS!

Wolf

- WITHOUT needing to be provoked, Wolves will attack Sheep, Rabbits, Foxes and even Baby Skeletons! Brave little fellas!

- WHEN angry, Wolves will let out a constant growling sound. So you know to keep your distance! They also have scary red eyes.

- ONCE you have a tamed pet Wolf, if it goes for a walk and gets more than 12 blocks away from you it will teleport back to your side.

GAMES MASTER PRESENTS
MINECRAFT TIPS CARDS!

Sugar

- EVERYONE knows that Horses like Sugar. Feed a Horse a Sugar lump in Minecraft and you will heal it by one point.

- MIX together Wheat, Sugar, Milk and Eggs on a Crafting Table and you will soon have yourself a rather yummy Cake!

- YOU can speed up the rate as which your Horses have baby foals by feeding them Sugar. Maybe the extra energy gets them going!

GAMES MASTER PRESENTS
MINECRAFT TIPS CARDS!

Diamond

- MINING Diamond Ore with an Iron or Diamond Pickaxe will give one Diamond. Enchant the Pickaxe with Fortune to get more!

- SHIPWRECK Treasure Chests are a good source of Diamonds, along with Stronghold Altar Chests and Nether Fortress Chests.

- YOU can select powers from Beacons using Diamonds too. Just put a Diamond in the slot when selecting an available power.

GAMES MASTER PRESENTS
MINECRAFT TIPS CARDS!

Minecart with TNT

- WHEN a Minecart with TNT explodes, it will bounce off any other Minecarts nearby, creating a fun effect!

- IF a speeding Arrow hits a Minecart with TNT it will cause a different sized explosion depending on how fast the arrow was travelling.

- WHILE a Minecart with TNT is classed as a vehicle, we do not recommend going for a ride, not unless you have brown trousers on.

GAMES MASTER PRESENTS
MINECRAFT TIPS CARDS!

Sweet Berries

- THE houses in the Taiga biome often have Sweet Berries piled up in stacks of 1-7 in their Chests, so it's worth opening them all up!

- PLANT a bunch of Sweet Berry Bushes around some animals and they will act like a barrier as the bushes hurt the animal if touched.

- FOXES are a fun new addition to Minecraft. Feed a fox some Sweet Berries and you will encourage it to breed, creating baby foxes!

GAMES MASTER PRESENTS
MINECRAFT TIPS CARDS!

Shield

- IF you break your Shield in a battle, don't worry it can be repaired! Take it to an Anvil with some spare Planks and it will be good as new!

- INCOMING attacks from enemies can be blocked using a Shield. While using one though, you will slow down to a sneaking pace.

- WANT to look as cool in battle as a Game of Thrones character? Craft your wood and iron with a Banner containing your pattern.

Golden Chestplate
ARMOUR

THERE are five types of Chestplate in Minecraft: leather, chainmail, iron, diamond and gold. But the most impressive when walking into battle has to be the Golden Chestplate. Everyone likes a bit of bling!

Bone Meal
UTILITY

YOU can fertilize most plants in Minecraft with Bone Meal. Spread some around the basic grass blocks you find and you will soon have incredible tall grass, or maybe even flowers to show off!

Skeleton Skull
DECOR

THINK of the Skeleton Skull as more of a cosplay bit of fun, rather than a useful block in Minecraft. These mob heads are for decoration only and come in Zombie, Skeleton, Wither Skeleton, Creeper and Dragon styles!

Underwater TNT
BLOCK

INTRODUCED in the Aquatic update of Minecraft in May 2018, Underwater TNT is needed if you want to create an explosion... well... underwater! Regular old TNT just can't be lit underwater you see!

Explorer Map
ITEM

EVERYONE loves a treasure hunt, right? In Minecraft you can find what are known as 'generated structures'. Places like woodland mansions, monuments and buried treasure using an Explorer Map!

Parrot
MOB

CHECK out the Jungles if you want to encounter Minecraft Parrots in the wild! These brightly coloured birds can be tamed, as you can see above where Alex has taught two of them to sit on her shoulders!

Crossbow
WEAPON

THE ranged weapon Crossbow can use either arrows or fireworks as ammunition. Firing fireworks around is great fun – but incredibly dangerous! As they say... don't try this at home kids!

Rotten Flesh
FOOD

IF you get really hungry and there is no food around, you can always tuck into some Rotten Flesh! It will fill your belly up, but you need to know something important – you may get food poisoning from it!

Brown Dye
DYE

BROWN is the colour you get if you mix all other colours together! In Minecraft you can make yourself Brown Dye by using Cocoa Beans. It can be used to colour all kinds of things from Sheep to Fireworks!

Games Master PRESENTS

MINECRAFT TIPS CARDS!

Skeleton Skull

- IF a Charged Creeper explodes and kills a Skeleton nearby, its head will be left behind to be picked up and used for fun!

- SIMILAR to Signs, you can place Skeleton Heads on blocks in 16 directions.

- THE most fun to be had with a Skeleton Head is to simply wear it! You will look like you are off to a Halloween party as you set off on your next Minecraft adventure.

Games Master PRESENTS

MINECRAFT TIPS CARDS!

Bone Meal

- USING Bone Meal helps virtually anything grow. If you splash some around underwater on a non-transparent block you will get seagrass.

- IF you are really lucky when using Bone Meal underwater you will get some Coral growing instead!

- ARE you a big fan of Mushrooms? Then try some Bone Meal on those – you will create fantastic giant mushrooms to feed the family!

Games Master PRESENTS

MINECRAFT TIPS CARDS!

Golden Chestplate

- YOU need 8 Gold Ingots to craft yourself a Golden Chestplate, and if you have two damaged ones you can craft them together to make one good one.

- NETHER Fortress Chests have a 19% chance of including a Golden Chestplate.

- A Golden Chestplate gives the same amount of protection in battle as Chainmail – 5 damage points. Well worth having!

Games Master PRESENTS

MINECRAFT TIPS CARDS!

Parrot

- YOU will find Parrots living in pairs in the wild, so if you tame one, tame the other or it will be sad!

- AS you would expect, Parrots spend a lot of their time just flying around the game. If you strike them, they will fly up, but eventually get tired and come back down to the ground.

- IF you would like a Parrot as a pet you need to feed it Seeds. Once you have a tamed Parrot, you can get it to sit by right-clicking on it!

Games Master PRESENTS

MINECRAFT TIPS CARDS!

Explorer Map

- THE big question is where on earth can you find an Explorer Map? A good place to try is by talking to Cartographer Villagers. They will sell them for a Compass and 12 Emeralds.

- CHECK Underwater Ruins Chests – these contain Buried Treasure Maps nearly 50% of the time.

- ONCE you discover treasure using a map, you will be rewarded with the Treasure Hunter achievement.

Games Master PRESENTS

MINECRAFT TIPS CARDS!

Underwater TNT

- THESE TNT blocks act pretty much like any regular TNT block and will explode anything around them – except for lava.

- YOU need Sodium and a regular TNT block to craft yourself some Underwater TNT.

- UNDERWATER TNT can be broken using any tool you have to hand, or even just by bashing it. You have to be a very brave Minecrafter to just bash a block of TNT though!

Games Master PRESENTS

MINECRAFT TIPS CARDS!

Brown Dye

- COMBINING Brown Dye with Gunpower and a Feather will give you a special kind of Firework Star!

- ADDING the dye to a tamed Wolf will not colour the Wolf brown – that would be cruel. Instead it will colour their collars.

- IF you find yourself with lots of Brown Dye, it's good to know you can stack them 64 blocks high! That's a lot of Brown Dye though – maybe try another colour?

Games Master PRESENTS

MINECRAFT TIPS CARDS!

Rotten Flesh

- SO where does someone get Rotten Flesh from? Well certain dead creatures in Minecraft will drop Rotten Flesh – try Zombies, Husks, Zombie Villagers or the Drowned.

- ANOTHER source of Rotten Flesh is while you are fishing. If you're not having much luck with the fish – you may hook some yummy flesh!

- IF you have a tamed Cat in your world, you may get a special Rotten Flesh gift from them!

Games Master PRESENTS

MINECRAFT TIPS CARDS!

Crossbow

- YOU can craft yourself a Crossbow by using a Stick, an Iron Ingot, some String and a Tripwire Hook.

- CROSSBOWS can also be found naturally occuring in the world – check out a pillager outpost watchtower chest – you might just get lucky!

- USING a crossbow is much like using a bow and arrow, but it takes much longer to load! Beware – Enderman can't be shot with one!

Leather Cap
ARMOUR

THE weakest of all the headgear you can wear in battle but the Leather Cap is better than nothing! Try upgrading to a chainmail helmet, iron helmet, diamond helmet, gold helmet or turtle shell.

Firework Rocket
CRAFTED

NOT only do Fireworks look great at a night-time party, they can also be used in Minecraft to propel the leathery wings Elytra along through the sky or fired from a crossbow to become a deadly weapon.

Clock
INFO

CLOCKS in Minecraft display the current time in the game by using the position of the sun and the moon in the sky relative to the horizon. If you are hiding away from scary mobs, it's useful to know when you can come out!

Dark Prismarine
BLOCK

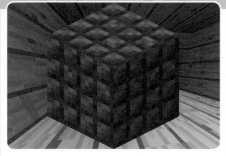

DECORATIVE blocks come in all colours and patterns, so your only limit in Minecraft is your imagination. Dark Prismarine is dark green in colour with a tight checked pattern on each side.

Ocelot Spawn Egg
ITEM

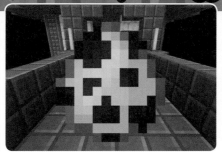

ANY mobs can be spawned into place in Minecraft using their Spawn Egg. They come in a wonderful range of colours and patterns – the Ocelot Spawn Egg is yellow with dark spots... following the colouring of the Ocelot!

Turtle
MOB

INTRODUCED in the Aquatic Update of Minecraft, Turtles have the rare ability to be able to move on land and in the sea. They are passive mobs and always friendly, so if you see one stop to say hello!

Gunpowder
WEAPON

MAKING things go "BANG!" in Minecraft needs Gunpower. It is an essential ingredient for any explosion. But where can you get it? Those nasty mobs Creeper, Ghasts and Witches will drop some when killed.

Cocoa Beans
FOOD

YOU'VE read Charlie and the Chocolate Factory, right? Then you will know just how essential Cocoa Beans are as a food ingredient! The essential part of making chocolate Cookies – a favourite snack!

Acacia Sapling
BLOCK

SAPLINGS are blocks like any other, but they are not solid, so you can walk through them. You will find the Acacia Saplings spawning naturally in Savanna village libraries. They are light green with brown branches.

GAMES MASTER PRESENTS
MINECRAFT TIPS CARDS!

Clock

- CRAFT yourself a Clock using four Gold Ingots and Redstone Dust, or you can sometimes find a Clock in a shipwreck map chest.
- THE Clock works by showing you the position of the sun and the moon on the dial.
- IT'S time for bed when the Clock shows you it is dusk – halfway between noon and midnight. Best not to sleep in The End or Nether though – clocks don't work there.

GAMES MASTER PRESENTS
MINECRAFT TIPS CARDS!

Firework Rocket

- BASIC Rockets without any colour explosion can be created by crafting Paper and Gunpowder. Up to three Gunpowders can be used to increase the power of the Rocket.
- ADDING an item called a Firework Star to the crafting mix will add colours to your Firework Rocket.
- ALL of the Firework Stars will explode at the same time creating amazing firework effects in the sky all around!

GAMES MASTER PRESENTS
MINECRAFT TIPS CARDS!

Leather Cap

- CRAFT yourself a Leather Cap by combining seven Leather animal skins together on a Crafting Table.
- TWO damaged Leather Caps can be combined together to make one good one.
- REGULAR Leather Caps can also be found occuring naturally in the world, try looking in village tannery chests. There are also Enchanted Leather Caps to be found in shipwreck supply chests.

GAMES MASTER PRESENTS
MINECRAFT TIPS CARDS!

Turtle

- NATURALLY spawning Turtles are found on beaches, usually in groups of up to five – 10% of these will be little baby Turtles!
- JUST like real-life Turtles, in Minecraft they are slow moving on land, but can move at incredible speed under water!
- WANT a Turtle to follow you? Then you need to be holding some Seagrass. They just can't get enough of this tasty stuff.

GAMES MASTER PRESENTS
MINECRAFT TIPS CARDS!

Ocelot Spawn Egg

- YOU can only use Spawn Eggs to summon mobs if you are in Creative Mode, or use a Summon command.
- SHOULD you summon a hostile mob into existence while playing in peaceful difficulty mode, they will be instantly deleted from the world.
- USE a Spawn Egg on the adult version of some passive mobs and rather than spawn a clone of itself, it will spawn a baby! Ahhh... little baby mobs are fun!

GAMES MASTER PRESENTS
MINECRAFT TIPS CARDS!

Dark Prismarine

- OBTAINING Dark Prismarine is done with a Pickaxe, it is the rarer form of Prismarine found only in ocean monuments.
- GOLD block rewards in ocean monuments appear as eight block groups – you will find the Dark Prismarine surrounding the gold blocks.
- IF you can't find any natural Dark Prismarine you can craft some with 8 Prismarine Shards and an Ink Sac.

GAMES MASTER PRESENTS
MINECRAFT TIPS CARDS!

Acacia Sapling

- ANY tool can be used to chop down an Acacia Sapling. They will drop blocks of wood when chopped.
- SAPLINGS will grow into fully sized trees if you plant them in an area that has at least six spaces above.
- BONE Meal can be used to speed up the growth of any sapling, or if you don't have enough light.
- THERE are many uses for saplings – for fuel, decoration, building and composting.

GAMES MASTER PRESENTS
MINECRAFT TIPS CARDS!

Cocoa Beans

- COCOA Pods are where you will get Cocoa Beans – they can be found naturally in Jungle biomes.
- PODS have three stages of growth, changing colour as they grow. If you harvest them too early you will only get one Cocoa Bean – you can get up to three in one go.
- BONUS Chests in the console versions of Minecraft will contain a Cocoa Bean half of the time – so be sure to check out the contents!

GAMES MASTER PRESENTS
MINECRAFT TIPS CARDS!

Gunpowder

- NATURALLY occuring Gunpowder can be found in many of the game's chests. Try looking inside shipwreck supply chests, dungeon chests, desert temple chests and woodland mansion chests where it is found in varying amounts.
- THE list of things you can make with Gunpowder is long. Try a Firework Rocket, Firework Star, Fire Charge, TNT or a Splash Potion for throwing at your enemies.

FOOD — Dried Kelp

NEED a quick snack to satisfy you before going off on a Minecraft adventure or into battle? Then Dried Kelp is for you! It is known to be the quickest acting foodstuff in Minecraft. Munch away!

POTION — Splash Potion

YOU can't really ask your enemies to kindly eat some poison so you can win a battle. That's where Splash Potions come in. You can brew them and throw them at your enemies, with the potion affecting them immediately.

WEAPON — Trident

IF fighting in melee or ranged combat is your thing then the Trident is the perfect weapon for you. You can use the enchantment Loyalty to make a thrown Trident return to you too!

BLOCK — Brain Coral

TEN types of Coral can be found under the water in the Aquatic Update of Minecraft. Brain Coral is one of these and comes in regular and dead versions. It's called Brain Coral because of its pink colour.

ITEM — Ghast Tear

GHASTS will drop one of their Tears when you kill them. Now you feel really bad for doing it, don't you?! It's an essential part of obtaining this powerful brewing ingredient though, so don't feel too sad.

MOB — Salmon

INTRODUCED in the Aquatic Update along with lots of other cool fish, Salmon are common mobs found in oceans and rivers. They will spawn 12-32 blocks away – you will spot them as they are very long!

TOOL — Diamond Hoe

ESSENTIAL for any budding Minecraft farmer, a Hoe is needed to work on the land, turning regular Grass blocks and Dirt into farmland that you can sew seeds in to generate a harvest.

FOOD — Cookie

WHO doesn't love the occasional cookie, eh? They are a quick and convenient snack in Minecraft, but just like in real life they do not restore very much hunger or saturation. We'll just have to have one more...

TOOL — Lead

IF you've got a passive mob around your Minecraft homestead that you want to take on walks, you're going to need a Lead! The obvious ones are the Wolf and Pig, but you can also put a Lead on a Llama!

GAMES MASTER PRESENTS

MINECRAFT TIPS CARDS!

Trident

- YOU cannot craft a Trident in the game, they can only be obtained as a dropped item from a Drowned.
- DROWNED are a special kind of Zombie that has... well drowned in the ocean. It's not just friendly Dolphins and Turtles down there – there are nasties lurking too!
- A thrown Trident deals eight damage points in one blow – which is mighty impressive for a weapon. It also does not slow down in water.

GAMES MASTER PRESENTS

MINECRAFT TIPS CARDS!

Splash Potion

- SPLASH Potions are created by brewing together a regular Potion with some Gunpowder.
- UNLIKE regular potions where you can recycle the bottle when you have used it, with Splash Potions the bottle is destroyed when you throw it at your enemies.
- CAULDRONS can be filled with the potion you want to use as a Splash Potion – then using a bottle on the cauldron will fill it ready for action.

GAMES MASTER PRESENTS

MINECRAFT TIPS CARDS!

Dried Kelp

- DRYING Kelp to make this tasty snack is a simple matter of crafting natural Kelp with any fuel in a furnace.
- COMBINING nine Dried Kelp items together on a Crafting Table you will make yourself a Dried Kelp Block, making storing the ingredient much more convenient.
- BLOCKS of Dried Kelp also make fantastic fuel sources – it can smelt 20 times from one block.

GAMES MASTER PRESENTS

MINECRAFT TIPS CARDS!

Salmon

- THERE are small, normal and large sizes of Salmon in Minecraft – which one you go for depends on how hungry you are!
- KILLING a Salmon with fire gives you... cooked Salmon! Perfect for barbecues!
- LIKE most fish, Salmon swim around in schools. There can be up to six Salmon in a school and these clever fish can swim up waterfalls that are 4-5 blocks high!

GAMES MASTER PRESENTS

MINECRAFT TIPS CARDS!

Ghast Tear

- BREW together a Ghast Tear with a Water Bottle and you will create a Mundane Potion. This potion is the essential starting point for more interesting potions.
- AN Awkward Potion brewed with a Ghast Tear will create a Potion of Regeneration that will restore your health when drunk.
- CRAFTING a Ghast Tear with Glass and Eye of Ender will make an End Crystal, normally found in The End.

GAMES MASTER PRESENTS

MINECRAFT TIPS CARDS!

Brain Coral

- WARM Oceans are the place to look for all kinds of Coral. It comes in tube, brain, bubble, fire and horn varieties.
- GROWING Coral needs warm water biomes and Bone Meal, used on dirt, coarse dirt, sand, red sand or gravel blocks.
- TAKING Coral out of the water turns it into Dead Coral. Coral needs to be touching water on one side to survive.

GAMES MASTER PRESENTS

MINECRAFT TIPS CARDS!

Lead

- WITH a mob on a Lead, using the Lead on a nearby Fence will tie them to it!
- SHOULD the mob fight and struggle on a Lead, it will stretch up to 10 Blocks away before it snaps!
- SET up a caravan of Llamas in any of the console versions of Minecraft, five in a row, using Leads and you will earn yourself a special achievement called "So I Got That Going for Me".

GAMES MASTER PRESENTS

MINECRAFT TIPS CARDS!

Cookie

- TWO blocks of Wheat and one of Cocoa Beans will allow you to craft a Cookie!
- NEVER give a Parrot a Cookie! If you do they will die instantly and start giving off a Poison as chocolate it actually poisonous to parrots!
- COOKIES were first introduced to Minecraft way back in 2011 when they were the only stackable food in the game.

GAMES MASTER PRESENTS

MINECRAFT TIPS CARDS!

Diamond Hoe

- WHEREAS a regular wooden Hoe will last for 60 uses, the Diamond Hoe is extra durable and can be used 1,562 times before it breaks!
- YOU can find yourself a Diamond Hoe by exploring in Woodland Mansion Chests.
- TWO nuggets of Diamond and two Sticks are needed to make a Diamond Hoe on a Crafting Table. They can be used as weapons as well as for farming.

PUZZLES

Test your brain with these teasers...

SPOT THE DIFFERENCE

TAKE A look at these two photos of Alex, Steve and their pet pig Percy dancing with their friends! Can you spot the 6 differences between the two photos? Here's a clue... Creepers have two eyes!

1

CIRCLE ALL THE DIFFERENCES ON PHOTO 2!

2

ANSWERS ON PAGE **93**

MINECRAFT'S CRAZIEST EASTER EGGS!

Rainbow sheep and killer bunnies? You've got to be yolking! We've compiled the craziest Minecraft Easter Eggs into one super-crazy feature!

Easter is, as everybody knows, a most sacred time of year. Easter is about sacrifice. It's about rebirth. It's about the holy ritual of shoving novelty chocolate into your cake-hole until your nose starts to leak whatever it is they put in Creme Eggs (paradise goo? Liquid unicorn? Best not to ask). Of course, Easter's really about easter eggs – and by that we mean hidden secrets, not actual eggs – and Minecraft's got loads of them stuffed inside its ravines. But like all good things in Minecraft, they're buried beneath the surface, revealing their delicious mysteries to only the most persistent pickaxes...

Too busy battling a serious case of the chocolate sweats to move? No matter – we've dug through every crevice of code to bring you Minecraft's super-secret treats. And what did we find on our easter egg hunt? Upside-down animals! Encrypted puzzles! Spelling errors! Barefaced lies! Other things you probably don't want to put in your mouth! And most of all, hilarious hacks that remind us why Minecraft is so very sweet.

But don't be April Fooled: some of the rumours you've heard about are total tosh, so we've supplied a guide to which easter eggs are the real deal and which ones are... ahem... eggs-aggerated. Crack on!

1

TRUE!

CHISELLED GOOD LOOKS

Take a moment out of your hectic, world-domination-oriented schedule to actually look at what you're using to build that terrifying obelisk monument to yourself. Grab a chunk of chiseled sandstone in your blocky hands (it's two sandstone slabs stacked on top of each other), and take a squiz at it. Closer. Clooooooser. Not that close, you're getting drool on it. Back up a little, and check out those two shady little blobs right in the middle, complete with droopy mouth underneath. Yup, that's a Creeper face alright. Who knows how Minecraft's most famous mob wormed his way into the sandstone block texture, but his 'orrible mug is unmistakably there. And if that wasn't suspicious enough for you, chiseled red sandstone is quite clearly harbouring the spooky, three-skulled shadow of the wither. Now you can rest easy in the knowledge that your empire is built from the petrified corpses of your enemies. Hardcore.

2

LOADING WITH A CHANCE OF MEAT-BOATS

Okay, so the sweet stuff isn't for everyone. Fortunately, there is a savoury easter egg hidden deep within Minecraft's code. So deep, in fact, that this particular menu screen mishap only has a 0.01% chance of floating to the surface every time you boot up the game. Even though it's spelled out in huge cobblestone letters, only the keenest of peepers will notice the game's title appearing as the jumbled-up "MINCERAFT" once in a blue moon. We've only heard legends of this tasty typo. But if you're convinced it's just a tall tale, you'd be wrong. Notch confirmed the easter egg's existence on the Minecraft subreddit back in 2013, calling the butchered title an "old running gag" and part of the never-ending quest to "hide stuff in plain sight" in his game. Good to know that this one was an intentional misteak (that's a pun and an anagram. You're welcome.)

MINCERAFT
Treatment for your face

Singleplayer

Multiplayer

Texture Packs

Options...   Quit Game

TRUE!

3

OUT OF THEIR GOURDS

TRUE!

Sometimes, the world can get too much. It can't be easy, being a Minecraft mob and having to share your turf with a bunch of other baddies. Perhaps that's why each Hallowe'en, many skellybobs, zombies and creepers hide their heads inside pumpkins and jack o'lanterns for the night. This easter egg isn't just adorably spooky – it can actually be very useful if you're well-prepared for October 31st. Upgrade a tool with a Looting enchantment, get cracking those scary skulls, and you'll find that the veggie visors will plop right off enemy heads and into your inventory. Quite apart from the visual appeal of the pumpkin parade prancing through Minecraft's forests, there are definitely agricultural rewards to reap: with a savvy farming set-up in place, you'll be munching pumpkin pie (usually a rare delicacy) throughout the entirety of November. Whoever said easter eggs weren't part of a balanced diet?

4

FALSE!

STEVE-IL TWIN

You haven't heard of blocky hero Steve's demonic doppelganger? Oh boy. The first sighting of the anti-Steve came courtesy of Brocraft streamer Copeland's infamous video. He's rumoured to be symbolic of Notch's deceased brother, which would be enough to make us do a widdle in our iron boots... were it not for the fact that Notch has confirmed that he never had a brother. Awkward. Turns out the creepy tale is totally fabricated, and there's no source code that would ever spawn something like Herobrine. That hasn't stopped Mojang from fuelling our nightmares, however – the milky-eyed topiarist has repeatedly popped up in official art, and is referenced in every set of patch notes. It's false (at least, we're pretty sure. Oh No.).

5

TRUE!

ALPHABET GET!

Those odd little symbols that whizz about the table when you're riffling through your bumper book of enchantments don't half look mysterious and impressive. But they're far from random squiggles: they're actually part of the Standard Galactic Alphabet. Tom Hall dreamed up the simple code for his Commander Keen series of videogames on MS-DOS in the early '90s. Each symbol corresponds to one of the 26 letters of the alphabet, meaning that it's possible to decipher coded words in some of the enchantments you perform on your various bludgeoning bits and bobs. The enchantment names are randomly generated, so most are likely to be utter nonsense, but that doesn't mean you can't freak out your friends with your knowledge of this easter egg. "Hm," you'll announce, visibly consulting your SGA chart and stroking your luxuriant beard, "The runes are telling me there's something green and explody in your near future..."

UNKNOWN!

6

CORE BLIMEY

They say the apple doesn't fall far from the tree. But what about the Notch? One of Minecraft's most discussed easter eggs is what exactly Papa Minecraft's character drops upon meeting a sticky end in the servers. Rumour has it that somewhere, buried in the game's code, is a command that produces a single, shiny red apple once a player manages to slay digi-Notch. The urban myth seems to have been generally accepted, although there's been no concrete evidence of such an event ever occurring. If it was once an easter egg, it was quickly patched out of the game, and now we have only the shaky testimony of those players lucky enough to have met their Minecraft maker. He's too busy swimming in an M&M-and-cash-filled infinity pool in Beverly Hills to make it online much anymore. Guess we'll have to find a more reliable source of making apple pies.

7

RABID RABBIT

TRUE!

It just wouldn't be Easter without fluffy bunnies. Sorry, did we say "fluffy"? We meant "killer". Killer bunnies. These cuddly little harbingers of doom are a reference to a scene from the film Monty Python and the Holy Grail, in which one flopsy little cottontail single-handedly takes down several armed men. Your diamond armour has no power here. The Killer Bunny used to be a rare natural spawn, but these days you'll need a command block to summon one into your game. We'd recommend extreme caution when doing so, as they've got a vicious streak a mile wide (by which we mean they do damage equal to that of withers. Ouch.) Pure white with red eyes – actually significantly less horrifying than their original blood-stained texture – and a crimson temper to match. TNT's probably your safest bet when fighting one, seeing as there's no Holy Hand Grenade in Minecraft.

Steve Co. Supply Crate

You need a Steve Co. Supply Crate Key to open this. You can pick one up at the Minecraft store.

Not now | Go to store

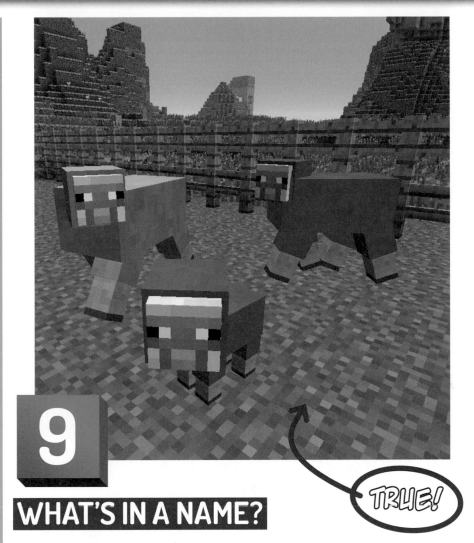

8

TRUE!

FOOL ME ONCE

We're breaking open some vintage Mojang trolling for this one. Rewind all the way back to April 1st, 2011, when every chunk generated between the first and the fifth of the month had a small chance of containing a locked chest. But it wasn't a locked chest, was it, Mojang? It was a regular ol' block with a fancy paint job, you monsters. Trying to open the Steve Co. Supply Crate would result in being forwarded on to the Minecraft Store, where if you decided to proceed to checkout with its ridiculous microtransactions, you'd be treated to a faceful of screeching Velociraptor. A midi version of the Rick Astley classic "Never Gonna Give You Up" was the bittersweet icing on the cake.

9

TRUE!

WHAT'S IN A NAME?

Shakespeare's Romeo and Juliet tried to teach us that when it comes to the crunch, names don't matter. Listen, bard-brain: us 'Crafters beg to differ. Renaming Minecraft's animals changes their very DNA, leading to some unique easter eggs. Hunt down a name tag, whip up an anvil and gather your motley crew of critters. Dubbing a humble sheep "jeb_" will cause it to turn into Disco Sheep, a highly-evolved mammal with a constantly colour-changing woolly coat and an insatiable appetite for Motown bangers. If you can't get down with the grooviest grass-muncher in town, there's an equally brilliant alternative. Name any mob "Dinnerbone" or "Grumm" (all these magical words are the nicknames of Mojang developers, by the way) and they'll instantly be flipped upside-down, their stubby little limbs flailing comically in the air as they go about their business none the wiser. Cow-flipping trumps cow-tipping any day of the week.

10

TRUE!

FACE IN THE MUSIC

You'll have done your fair share of digging if you're a tried-and-true player, but getting to the bottom of this mystery requires diamond-hard determination. For starters, you've got to get hold of a music disc – that means finding one at rare dungeon drop, or somehow convincing a skeleton to shoot and kill a creeper – and it needs to be Music Disc 11. That's the strange, broken-looking one that plays one minute and eleven seconds of someone breathing heavily while running away from an unknown danger. No, don't set fire to it, we need it for science! Root around in your game's Minecraft folders and grab the disc's .ogg file. Next, run it through spectrogram software to reveal... well, just look at it. It doesn't take much to spot the Minecraft-esque face and the numbers 1241. There are endless theories on what this could mean. We're carefully ignoring the fact that the face looks like Herobrine's.

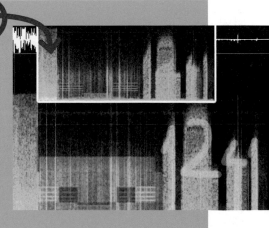

11

FOOL ME TWICE

A Minecraft April Fools' shenanigan made creepers even more... creepy. The 1.10 build (hang on, what happened to 1.9?!) was entitled the "Love and Hugs Update". Creepers blew kisses instead of holes in buildings; harming any living being was completely impossible; zombies became super-cuddly; minecarts got a fluffy pink interior; nasty lava was replaced with liquid cheese. It was all terribly progressive... but things got progressively more terrible when we discovered that we couldn't ride horses, Mojang gleefully deeming it "unfair" to the animals. We all breathed huge sighs of relief once normal, meanie Minecraft service resumed – although we would have been perfectly happy to hang onto those lakes of fondue.

12

HACK 'N' SPLASH

TRUE!

On logging into the game, you're always greeted by a "splash" slapped over the game's title – that is, a sunny yellow message in Minecraft's trademark pixelated font. Witty references to gaming and geekery abound, but there are some even more cool easter eggs that can pop up from time to time. For instance, firing up the game on 1st June (a.k.a. our glorious creator's cake-day) prompts the "Happy birthday, Notch!" splash to appear. Aww, Minecraft – you shouldn't have! Even more intriguingly, there's a nod to Pokémon buried deep within that splash code. Uncover the hidden reference by dipping into your Minecraft folders and deleting the one named splash.txt, making sure not to delete META-INF before that. The splash then changes to "missingno" – as in, the famous glitch species of Pokémon that can be found in the first generation of the game.

13

MOJANGLED BANNER

TRUE!

You might have already twigged that you can make a rather fetching pair of creeper curtains out of banners and some of those disembodied heads you've got lying around the place. But did you know that your interior could be repping the mighty Mojang? This secret crafting recipe will have you tearing down those ugly drapes and plastering the indie developer's logo all over the show. Rustle up your standard banner out of six blocks of wool and a stick. Next, it's time to find an enchanted golden apple. Well, nobody said a complete style overhaul was going to be easy. Mashing the two together in a crafting grid will create a snazzy Mojang banner: you can even include dye to match your potted plants! Yes, those Notch apples will cost you a pretty penny in gold – but you can't put a price on good taste, darling.

UNKNOWN!

14

FAR, FAR AWAY

Minecraft and ill-advised exploration go hand in hand, so it wasn't long before the most intrepid players pushed the limits of their infinitely-generated environments. They packed their inventories to the brim with pork chops and pickaxes, venturing an epic 12.5 million blocks away from spawn point and to the end of the world. Not The End – the real end of the Minecraft world, known as the Far Lands, where horrors far greater than nasty dragons rear their glitchy heads. Layers of ground and sky stack and float in between each other, and the secret borderlands are so broken that it's not actually your character who's moving around – the ground is moving underneath you while you remain perfectly still. (Ugh, pass us that iron bucket, would you?) Presumably, it's been patched out as of version 1.8, but incoming reports suggest that the accidental anti-biome is still wreaking physics-based havoc even further afield.

KNOW YOUR BIOMES
PLATEAU

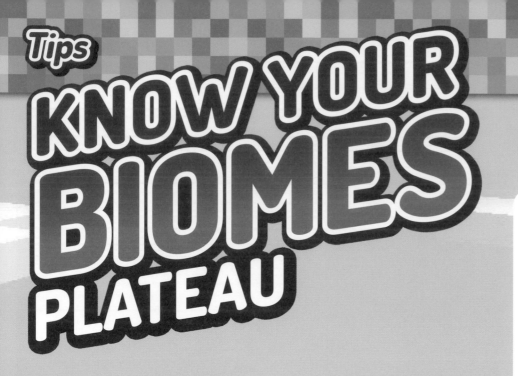

THIS VISUALLY STRIKING environment is an iconic upgrade of the hills biome, only with each hill boasting a flat bit at the top. Perfect for when you're after a location for a hilltop fort, a skull-shaped castle in the side of a mountain, or for building an easily spottable home base. You will have to devise a way to scale the sharp incline, though...

PLATEAUS ARE MOST IMPRESSIVE WHEN THEY ARE FOUND HYBRIDISED WITH MESA OR SAVANNA BIOMES.

MESA PLATEAUS CAN OCCASIONALLY HAVE EACH HILL SEPARATED BY SWATHES OF FLAT WASTELAND. THESE CAN BE TOUGH TO NAVIGATE AND TO KEEP AN EYE ON.

IF YOU PLAN ON BUILDING ON TOP OF A PLATEAU, BETTER BUILD A LADDER OR SOME STEPS TO HELP YOU WHEN GETTING UP AND DOWN. OR, IF YOU'RE A PRO, CRAFT YOURSELF A WORKING MINECART ESCALATOR.

PUZZLE ANSWERS

PAGE 20
CREEPER SEARCH

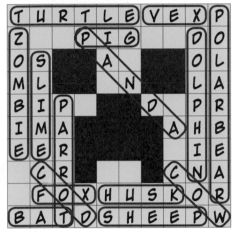

PAGE 21
DINNER TIME

The animals were eating...

= 🍪

= 🐟

= 🥔

= 🌿

= 🌾

= 🐟

PAGE 36
NAME THAT MOB

The pesky hostile mobs were:

1 = Slime　　2 = Ravager

3 = Guardian　　4 = Shulker

5 = Enderman　　6 = Magma Cube

7 = Skeleton

PAGE 37
LIGHTNING CODE

The secret phrase was "Minecraft was made by Notch"!

PAGE 58
WORD BLOCKS

1 = Glowstone, 2 = Fermented, 3 = Mooshroom,
4 = Polar Bear, 5 = Enchanted, 6 = Endermite.

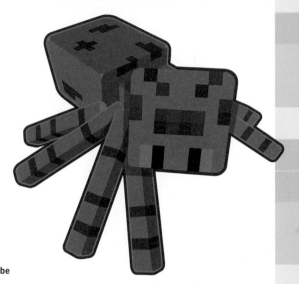

PAGE 83
SPOT THE DIFFERENCE

Here are the six differences: